The
BEATING ANXIETY
Workbook

Dr Stephanie Fitzgerald

Dedicated to Josie Jay

Dr Stephanie Fitzgerald is a clinical psychologist specializing in the treatment of anxiety disorders. As a BABCP accredited practitioner, Stephanie has successfully used cognitive behavioural therapy (CBT) to help those affected by anxiety to overcome the disorder and go on to live fuller lives, free from symptoms.

Stephanie sees anxiety as a bully and encourages her patients to stand up to that bully. Her approach to dealing with anxiety is practical, hands-on and boundaried, allowing individuals to regain control of their lives.

Stephanie has worked with many different anxiety disorders including, but not limited to, the disorders outlined in this book. Her previous book, *Teach Yourself: The CBT Workbook* (Hodder & Stoughton, 2013), outlines CBT techniques that can be applied to many different problems. CBT techniques can be used not only by those with a specific anxiety disorder but also by anyone who wants to know how to recognize and deal with their own anxieties, great or small.

The
BEATING ANXIETY
Workbook

Dr Stephanie Fitzgerald

First published in Great Britain in 2013 by Hodder & Stoughton. An Hachette UK company.

First published in US in 2013 by The McGraw-Hill Companies, Inc.

This edition published 2013

Copyright © Stephanie Fitzgerald 2013

Cover image © dibrova /Shutterstock

Typeset by Cenveo® Publisher Services.

Printed and bound in Great Britain by CPI Group (UK) Ltd, Croydon CRO 4YY.

Hodder & Stoughton policy is to use papers that are natural, renewable and recyclable products and made from wood grown in sustainable forests. The logging and manufacturing processes are expected to conform to the environmental regulations of the country of origin.

Hodder & Stoughton Ltd

338 Euston Road

London NW1 3BH

www.hodder.co.uk

Acknowledgements

I would like to say a big thank you to Victoria Roddam at Hodder & Stoughton for her help and guidance (about all things book and other!). It has been a real pleasure working together again.

I would also like to thank my patients who have all been brave enough to come with me on a journey to kick anxiety out of their lives. Overcoming anxiety can feel challenging, but the greatest reward of all is seeing my patients happy and healthy and living a full and enjoyable life free from anxiety. Well done and thank you to all of you who continue to make me proud of what I do.

Very special thanks must go to Professor Lars-Göran Öst who helped me conquer my long-standing fear of spiders in a single therapy session. It was a wonderful experience and I am thankful to him for his tremendous help and support.

Lastly, I would like to thank my friends and family who have put up with me being too busy to do anything lately. I hope you agree it was worth it!

Contents

How to use this book

This workbook from Teach Yourself ® includes a number of special features which have been developed to help you understand the subject more quickly and reach your goal successfully. Throughout the book, you will find these indicated by the following icons.

 Key ideas: to make sure you grasp the most important points.

 Spotlight: an important and useful definition explained in more depth.

 Exercise: designed to help you to work out where you are, where you want to be and how to achieve your goals. Exercises include:

 Writing exercises – fill in your answers in the space provided.

 Reflective exercises – think about the way you do things.

 Dig deeper: an exercise that offers further reflection or deeper explanations of the topic.

 Test yourself: assess yourself with questions about an aspect of the subject.

 Practice: put the ideas you learn about into practice.

 Quotes: inspiring and motivating you.

At the end of each chapter you will find:

 Summary: a section consolidating the main things you should remember from that chapter.

  What I have learned: helping you summarize for yourself what you can take away from each chapter.

 Where to next?: introducing you to the next step.

At the end of the book you will find:

  Worksheets and record sheets: help you highlight the key goals you want to achieve, the ways you can go about achieving them, and your thoughts as you go through the process.

Introduction

In this introduction you will learn:

▶ how this book will help you overcome anxiety, using a range of effective techniques that you will learn through doing a series of practical exercises

▶ how to use the workbook to develop your skills in reducing and managing anxiety that you can use anywhere

▶ the benefits you can expect once you have finished the book.

Anxiety is something that we are all familiar with and will experience at some stage in our lives. Unfortunately, in today's world, we cannot avoid a certain level of stress and anxiety. With increased pressures on our finances, our relationships, our work and our family situations, it is only natural that we have to deal with some level of anxiety at times.

This workbook focuses on general anxiety and also examines some specific anxiety problems that people often encounter, such as panic disorder, phobias, obsessive–compulsive disorder and generalized anxiety disorder. However, you don't need to have a diagnosed anxiety disorder in order to benefit from reading this workbook. The book contains a range of techniques based on cognitive behavioural therapy (CBT) to help you manage the anxiety that can creep into everyday living, as well as more severe anxiety problems.

If you've never heard of CBT before, don't worry. A clear explanation of all the techniques, how and why they work, and how to use them will be given as you work your way through the book. The idea of this workbook is that, as well as giving you the theory behind the techniques, you will also get practical guided exercises to help you to put some of that theory into practice.

'A day of worry is more exhausting than a day of work.'

John Lubbock

→ How will this book help me?

This workbook will help you identify the symptoms of your anxiety and understand where and how anxiety develops for you. Once you develop the skills of being able to identify the potential 'triggers' for your anxiety, this will help you to know when and why you may be feeling anxious. As well as teaching you how to identify those symptoms of anxiety and recognize when and where they occur, this workbook will teach you specific skills to be able to reduce and manage that anxiety effectively.

Rather than try to manage anxiety on your own, you will have this book as a companion on your journey to overcome your anxiety. It will offer you practical steps to help you through situations that you may have been avoiding as a result of your anxious feelings.

This book will also help you identify the kinds of behaviour that will have been maintaining that level of anxiety or keeping it going. Often we find ourselves doing things because they make us feel better and reduce our anxiety in the short term. For example, we may avoid something, someone or somewhere to stop ourselves worrying or becoming anxious. However, although the techniques we develop may make us feel better in the short term, they can be making the problem worse in the long term. This book gives you some alternative behaviours to try when you feel anxious, to help you break the cycle of some of those unhelpful maintaining behaviours.

→ How should I use this workbook?

Try to read the chapters in order, as each one will follow the last and build on the skills you developed and the information offered in previous chapters. This means that skipping ahead to chapters that may feel more relevant to you may not be helpful, as some of the content may not then make sense.

The exercises and tips within this book are designed to be practised and carried out alongside your everyday life. The idea is that you are developing skills that you can use anywhere. This means that you do not need to do anything special to prepare for using this workbook. What is helpful is to approach the exercises with an open mind and to remember that you may find some parts tougher than others – and that this is completely normal.

WHY ARE THERE SO MANY EXERCISES?

You'll notice that each chapter includes several exercises to complete. Although this may feel like a lot of work to do, the exercises encourage a more 'interactive' approach to the material offered and will make it more meaningful for you. Rather than just reading a book on the theory of why these activities or exercises work, you actually get to experience the results first hand.

As with all things, you may find some of the exercises easier, more applicable or more enjoyable than others, and that's fine. You may want to use every skill you learn in this book or find just one or two key skills that really work for you in overcoming your anxiety, or something in between. Every approach is equally valid; the main thing is that you work your way through the book and discover what works best for you when it comes to reducing your anxiety.

CAN I JUST DO THE EXERCISES AND FORGET THE REST?

The exercises will always be linked back to theory and so there will be a logical reason for why you need to complete them, so just doing the exercises on their own will not be helpful. They will not be meaningful or achieve the desired result on their own, as without knowing the theory behind them – which is clearly explained – you may find yourself struggling to develop these skills and fit them into your daily life.

I would recommend working your way through this book up to Chapter 6, and reading all the material and completing all the exercises, rather than skipping parts. You can skip Chapters 7 to 10, on specific anxiety disorders, if you think they don't apply to you, although by working through the book in its entirety you will notice greater benefits and a quicker development of your skills.

→ What can I expect once I've finished the book?

You can expect to feel more aware of when you experience anxiety, what causes it and what maintains anxiety in your own life. Alongside the recognition of your own anxiety, you will also feel equipped with the skills to deal with it.

Unfortunately, there is no way to guarantee an anxiety-free life. Often people say to me, 'I just want to stop worrying completely' but unfortunately this is unrealistic. There will be times when we experience life events or situations that cause us to become worried or anxious.

This applies to everyone, is perfectly natural and is just part of the world we live in today.

However, you will notice a significant reduction in your anxiety. You will feel confident in how to handle the anxiety and you will know the skills and techniques needed to prevent that anxiety causing you any distress or upset, or interfering with your day-to-day life. People often describe a feeling of 'taking control back' once they overcome their anxiety and it is an empowering experience.

'FEAR is an acronym in the English language for "False Evidence Appearing Real."'

Neale Donald Walsch

Summary

It is normal, healthy and part of our everyday world that we will sometimes experience understandable anxiety or worry in response to some situations.

This book will help you manage your own anxieties and equip you with the skills to overcome this anxiety, by taking a practical approach and using different exercises and techniques to help you apply the theory learned to your own life.

What I have learned

→ What are my thoughts, feelings and insights on what I have read so far?

nervous this book won't work. Read the book in its entirty, do all excercises even if they don't seem to apply.

Use the space below to summarize any actions you identify as a result of reading this introduction.

do all excercises. Stay open minded.

Where to next?

From this point you will begin to learn some of the techniques and skills discussed above. Your journey along a less anxious path starts here – good luck!

1 *What is anxiety?*

In this chapter you will learn:

▶ what we mean by anxiety, what symptoms of anxiety we experience and how to identify them

▶ about the role that anxiety plays in our own lives

▶ how we feel about our anxiety and how it bullies us into feeling we are not in control of our lives.

→ What do we mean by 'anxiety'?

Worried. Stressed. Frazzled. Overwrought. People have many different names for the emotions that can sit around anxiety. So what do we actually mean when we talk about being anxious?

Feeling anxious is how we feel when we are unable to stop thoughts that cause us concern or worry coming into our minds. As these thoughts increase, so our anxiety builds.

There are specific types of thoughts that people have when they are anxious. You may recognize some of them when you do the following exercise.

> '*Worrying is like a rocking chair, it gives you something to do, but it gets you nowhere.*'
>
> Glenn Turner

🕐 Exercise 1

 IDENTIFYING ANXIOUS THOUGHTS

Look at some of the thoughts below and circle any that seem particularly relevant to you or that you recognize as similar to your own anxious thoughts.

→ # But what *is* anxiety and why do I have it?

Anxiety is a bully. It's as simple as that. It's a big, messy, chaotic bully, which tries to creep into every part of our lives and our minds until we are constantly anxious. Anxiety feeds off itself. Therefore the more anxious and the more worried we are, the bigger and stronger our anxiety will be. There are many reasons why people develop anxiety. Highlighting where your own anxiety develops is important and this will be addressed later in this book.

2

It's important to start to view anxiety as separate from yourself. It may sound strange but it's helpful to recognize the anxiety as something separate from you. It is not the case that you are 'an anxious person' but that you are 'a person with anxiety'. This change in phrasing may sound like splitting hairs but understanding the difference plays a huge part in overcoming your anxiety.

Part of the process of overcoming anxiety is to recognize when it is bullying you and learning how to challenge and stand up to the anxiety. This may sound scary but, like all bullies, anxiety is actually a coward. Once you are equipped with the right tools, you will know exactly how to stand up to your anxiety and, even though it may not feel like it right now, you *are* stronger than your anxiety and you *will* overcome this. Beginning to see yourself as separate from your anxiety is an important first step in overcoming it and one that you can start on straight away.

→ Worry or anxiety: what's the difference?

Anxiety and worry can be considered to be different from each other. Some people consider their 'worry' to be their thought or concern that they think about and the 'anxiety' to be the resulting emotion that comes with this worry. However, many people use the terms worry and anxiety interchangeably and so for the purposes of this book you will notice both worry and anxiety being discussed and used in this way, in order to help people relate to the ideas being talked about.

In terms of whether you consider yourself to worry or to have anxiety, do not get bogged down in the language. The techniques outlined in this book are designed to help with both worries and anxieties and you will be able to apply them to both, however you recognize your concerns.

→ If I'm a worrier, am I anxious too?

Many people describe themselves as being 'a bit of a worrier'. This often takes the form of expecting the worst outcome, or worrying about situations or events that never happen, for example an imagined confrontation with someone or expecting bad news that never comes.

There is nothing inherently wrong with being a bit of a worrier. Often, when we consider situations, it may be natural for anxious or worrying thoughts to pop into our minds. This is particularly common when the situation or event is important or significant in some way. For example, it would be natural to worry a bit more when organizing a wedding than when organizing a casual barbecue for a few friends. This is because the greater the responsibility we feel, the more anxious we become. More on that later!

WHY DOES IT MATTER IF I'M ANXIOUS?

Anxiety in some situations is natural and healthy. For example, if we are in a situation we perceive as dangerous, the anxiety we feel about this danger will provide our bodies with a small shot of adrenaline. This adrenaline, in the short term, is very helpful. It keeps us alert and provides us with a good instinct about whether to leave or stay in that situation. This is an evolutionary process designed to keep us safe, known as our 'fight or flight' response.

However, do not be lulled into a false sense of security by thinking that this means that anxiety is good for you. In the long term, too much adrenaline is unhealthy. By remaining consistently anxious, we can be exposed to too much adrenaline. This means we'll find it hard to relax, our appetite and sleep patterns will be affected, and we may even feel nausea or develop headaches and muscle tension. We may notice effects on our mood as well, becoming more irritable or easily rattled by situations that would not normally have affected us in such a way.

Remaining consistently anxious over a long period means we are not truly living in the moment. If you are constantly thinking ahead, planning the worst-case scenario and planning how to deal with this scenario (which, let's remember, hasn't even happened and may never happen), you are not going to be fully absorbing and enjoying the moment that you are in. By constantly thinking ahead, you will never be able simply to enjoy a situation.

Constant worry and anxiety can affect every part of our lives without us even realizing it. This may be because our anxiety is 'free-floating' and adapts and changes to worry about whatever we deal with, so we never relax. Alternatively, we may have one or two constant worries or anxieties that exhaust us and mean we are 'keyed up', tired, ratty and with no energy to enjoy the things we want to enjoy.

SURELY FEELING ANXIOUS HELPS ME?

Many people think that being slightly anxious about things helps them in some way. They feel that, by thinking through a worst-case scenario and planning for it, they are more prepared somehow and better able to face and deal with it. Some of this thinking ahead is normal, typical reasoning around a very likely situation, such as 'It looks as though it might rain... if it does, I'll move the picnic indoors.' This logical thinking ahead is not problematic and does not cause us anxiety.

However, constantly worrying about things that may never happen – and for which we have no evidence that they might happen – can lead to us feeling horribly anxious for no reason. For example, you may have continual worries about having a car accident. Elements of this situation are completely out of your control, such as the other drivers on the road, the weather and the driving conditions. Therefore this is a fairly pointless issue to worry about. You could spend hours every day thinking of all the different ways to avoid a car accident, but wouldn't you rather have those hours worry free? You may not even have an accident, and statistically you are unlikely to, so why worry about this and give yourself all the negative health effects of anxiety, by worrying over something you cannot control?

This is not a case of not taking sensible precautions or thinking ahead and planning; these are all perfectly normal thinking processes. The mistake people often make is feeling that their anxiety plays an important role, or makes them a better person in some way. Worrying about something can be mistaken for caring about something. We may consider that anxiety makes us a better person because worrying about something and preventing it happening, or changing something to make a situation better for someone, makes us feel we've gone the extra mile. However, this is often unnecessary, takes a lot of effort and is rarely rewarded, and it also keeps us in an unhealthy anxious state.

→ When anxiety takes over

Read through the following case study and think about whether this applies to your own situation.

Eleanor's story

Eleanor was struggling with acute anxiety and believed anxiety helped her be a better mother. She found herself constantly worrying that her children were safe. She rated herself as extremely anxious and went to great lengths to protect her children, e.g. keeping them away from germs (real and imagined) and closely monitoring their diet. When pregnant with her second child, Eleanor had dreamed that her children would be kidnapped, so she became hyper-vigilant about knowing where they were at all times.

Below is an example of a conversation with the therapist where Eleanor describes her anxiety and the role she feels this anxiety plays.

Therapist: When you become anxious about your children's safety, what worries go through your mind?

Eleanor: I start to worry about where they are. I think to myself, 'Are they still in school?', 'Has someone taken them?' and then I start to think of what I'll do and who I'll talk to if they're not there when I go to collect them.

Therapist: So do you know what you'd do if they weren't there?

Eleanor: Yes, I have a very detailed plan. I spend a lot of time thinking about it. I'd call my mum immediately and I have the name of the child protection officer at my local police station so I'd contact them immediately. I'd go on TV and do one of those appeals, you know, like on the news, asking for their safe return. I make a note every day of what they're wearing and carrying so they could be easily identified and I carry that with me on the school run so that I could give those details out straight away. There are loads of things I know I'd do if this happened. I've watched them on TV, on the news, when someone goes missing, and I've noted down what the police ask for so I would be able to answer their questions.

Therapist: You mentioned that you think about this a lot and it sounds as though you have planned your response to this situation very carefully. Have you ever needed to put this plan in place?

Eleanor: No.

Therapist: Have you ever thought you might need to put this plan in place?

Eleanor: Well, nothing has ever happened to them, thank goodness, so I've never needed to use this plan yet.

Therapist: Why is it important to have this plan, if you've never needed it?

Eleanor: I feel prepared. I feel as though, if the worst happened, I'm ready and armed to deal with it. I feel I'm keeping my children safe by having this plan.

Therapist: Do other parents have these plans, do you think?

Eleanor: I'm not sure. They should. They should know what they'd do if something bad happened. It's no use trying to think on the spot when you're all emotional. You need to have a plan that you can put into place straight away. I mentioned it to another parent once. She just looked at me like I was weird. She said, 'Why are you even thinking about such horrible things?'

Therapist: How did you respond to that? Why are you thinking about such horrible things when other parents don't seem to be?

Eleanor: I guess it hasn't occurred to them. They are silly, though. If something happened to my kids, then I'm prepared. I know exactly what to do. I could take control in that situation even though I'd be devastated. I wouldn't waste time dithering. I feel as though my kids would be found quickly because I know exactly what to do.

Therapist: Does worrying about this cause you any problems?

Eleanor: Yes, sometimes I can't sleep. I worry I've missed a detail of the plan, so I lie there and go over and over it. I can't relax if the kids are out with other people. I always go with them. Even if my mum and dad have them over, I say, 'Don't take them anywhere.' I try and keep the kids in the house as much as possible and, if they play outside, I have to be able to see them the whole time. I make excuses if they get invited to places where I think they won't be properly supervised or too many people may be there and they might get lost in the crowd. I don't really enjoy time with my children like other mums. I hate taking them to the park, and then I feel bad for keeping them in. But I just worry, you know? I try to be a good mum and, if that means keeping them safe and indoors, then I'm ok with that. I'd rather do that than have something bad happen to them.

Therapist: So it sounds as though the worry helps you in some ways?

Eleanor: Definitely. I feel more in control. Worrying makes me a better mum.

It's easy to see the role that Eleanor believed her anxiety played. However, by talking her through the anxiety and the role it played in her own life, it was apparent that her constant anxiety was having a negative impact on her and her ability to enjoy life, including time with her children. Also, far from keeping her children safe when out and about, she was instead not letting them out of her sight.

At a later session Eleanor said she was worried her children would hate her, as she never let them do anything. The constant anxiety didn't make her feel better. She just continued to worry and felt miserable and worried about the future.

 # Exercise 2

 ## IS *MY* ANXIETY A PROBLEM?

Look at the common symptoms of anxiety listed below and place a tick (√) next to any that seem relevant to you or that you have experienced yourself.

Symptoms	Tick
Finding yourself worrying excessively about things other people don't seem to	✓
Finding it difficult to control the worry	✓
Unable to distract yourself away from the worry	✓
Feeling restless, keyed up or on edge most of the time	✓
Becoming easily fatigued	✓
Difficulties with memory and concentration – finding that your mind goes blank or that you cannot focus	
Feeling irritable	✓
Muscle tension in your body – tension knots or aches	✓
Feeling sick	✓
Sleep disturbance – difficulty getting to sleep/waking early/disrupted sleep	✓
The worrying interferes with some aspects of your life, e.g. socializing, working	✓
Worry symptoms cannot be explained by anything else, e.g. medication	✓

If you ticked any of the symptoms of anxiety listed above, this would suggest that anxiety is affecting you in a negative way. However, even if none of the above symptoms fit with how you are feeling, you can still use the techniques in this book to help you manage anxiety-provoking and worrying situations. By doing so, even if your anxiety is not particularly problematic, you will be well equipped to deal with situations that may arise in the future and cause you the stress and other side effects associated with anxiety.

→ Can't I just stop worrying?

Many of my patients tell me that they wish their mind had an 'off' switch, so that they could enjoy some time where their mind wasn't racing and where they could completely relax. Sadly, there isn't an off switch and I cannot guarantee that you will never be worried or anxious again. This is because life continues to throw things at us that we weren't expecting and so we cannot plan for every eventuality – even though anxiety will try to do so. Also, as mentioned earlier, small doses of anxiety and the resulting adrenaline can be very helpful at times.

However, what the techniques outlined in this book will do is reduce the *distress* associated with the anxiety. This means that you will experience a 'normal' or typical level of anxiety that is appropriate to the situation. The day-to-day levels of high anxiety will cease to exist. The constant nagging doubts and overwhelming fears can be contained, controlled and removed from our thoughts so that we can get back to the business of enjoying life.

→ Am I more anxious than everyone else?

When we are feeling very anxious or cannot stop worrying, we may look around us and think that everyone else is just calmly getting on with life. We experience intense envy of their apparent ability to cope when we feel our own mind is racing with worries. However, we must remember that anxiety is often unseen. We may have strong physical symptoms, but the worrying and anxiety-provoking thoughts themselves happen in our minds, so they are not visible to the outside world. We should therefore never assume that everyone else is living a carefree life while we are burdened with anxieties.

The truth is that everyone, at some point in their life, will experience a significant period of worry or anxiety. This is usually linked to a life event or a significant change in status. For example, it is natural to experience anxiety if one is made redundant or moves house. That is because these are stressful situations where we often feel out of control, and this makes us feel anxious.

→ The false promise of control

One of the ways in which anxiety is most devious is that it seems to offer us a sense of control over situations or events that are in fact out of our control. For example, worrying about things that may or may not happen may allow us to think of solutions. This makes us feel more prepared for the unexpected. This, in turn, can temporarily reduce our anxiety and make us feel more in control.

However, this is just a powerful illusion that anxiety gives us to make us continue to worry. Anxiety feeds off our worries: it needs us to actively worry or it will cease to exist. This is why you will find that once you stop worrying about one situation or event, another worry will step in to replace it. This is anxiety's way of staying alive and active in our minds. As long as we're worrying, the anxiety is there.

The truth is we cannot control what happens to us. Life doesn't work that way. But we can control how we live our lives. We can either spend hours and hours worrying and feeling anxious about things that may not even happen or live in the moment and enjoy our lives, accepting that some things may happen which we cannot control. Living in the moment is so much healthier and so much more rewarding, and the aim of this book is to free you from your anxious thoughts so that you can overcome your anxiety and start enjoying life again.

→ Taking the first steps

In order to begin to overcome your anxiety, you need first to recognize your anxieties and worries and how they are affecting you. Many people experience anxiety physically, with tension, headaches, nausea or an upset stomach and diarrhoea, among many other symptoms.

Exercise 3

THE PHYSICAL EFFECTS OF ANXIETY

Consider the last time you were anxious. Take yourself back to a situation when you were worried about something, and then look at the diagram below and imagine it is your body.

Draw on the body where you recognize some of the effects that anxiety had on you physically. If you would find it easier, do this when you are in an anxious situation, to help you identify the symptoms more easily.

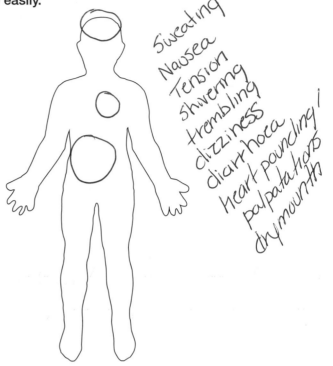

Some common physical symptoms of anxiety have been listed below to help you. If you recognize some of these symptoms, add them to the body drawing.

- Sweating ✓
- Nausea ✓
- Headaches
- Tension ✓
- Vomiting/retching
- Shivering ✓
- Trembling ✓

- Dizziness ✓
- Diarrhoea ✓
- Blurred vision
- Heart pounding/ ✓ palpitations
- Redness/flushing
- Dry mouth ✓

By looking at the way anxiety affects you physically, you will be better able to recognize the first warning signs of becoming anxious. This will act as your cue to address the anxiety and help you notice when anxiety is starting to affect you.

Now that we've identified how anxiety is affecting you physically, let's identify how anxiety is affecting you emotionally. This may sound strange, as anxiety is a feeling in itself. However, alongside the feelings of anxiety, we may notice other feelings that come up or warn us that we are anxious about something.

Exercise 4

THE EMOTIONAL EFFECTS OF ANXIETY

Look at the feelings listed below and tick the ones that apply to you. Then describe them more fully in the 'My feelings' column on the right. If you identify other feelings not listed here, add them to the list.

Common feelings	Tick	My feelings
Stressed	✓	stressed that I will never be able to work again
Tired	✓	exhausted all the time
Snappy		
Moody	✓	easily get upset
Irritable	✓	''
Overwhelmed	✓	maybe I won't be able to complete my days tasks
Tearful/emotional	✓	especially during pms
Unable to cope	✓	often feel hopeless
Panicky	✓	constantly afraid of "what ifs"
Unappreciated		
Depressed	✓	hopeless maybe i can't get better
Other	✓	afraid I'm dying / going to die
Other	✓	embarrassed to panic in public

Summary

1 Anxiety is a bully. In order to survive, it needs you to stay anxious and continue to worry about things.

2 You are separate from your anxiety. It is important to recognize that separation and start to see yourself as a person with anxiety rather than an anxious person.

3 Anxiety can be overcome. It needs addressing and challenging. Like all bullies, anxiety is a coward. Once we stand up to anxiety, it will stop bullying us and we can prevent ourselves feeling distressed by it.

What I have learned

→ What are my thoughts, feelings and insights on what I have read so far?

I like the interaction, keeps me focused.
I will remember that "anxiety is a bully"

Use the space below to summarize any actions you identify as a result of reading this chapter.

I need to stop giving my anxiety
power over me. I am not an anxious
person. My anxiety just bullies me often.

Where to next?

Now that we have identified the physical and emotional impact of your anxiety, we can start to consider the techniques used to address these. The next chapter introduces the techniques of cognitive behavioural therapy (CBT), describing how it works and showing how it can be used to overcome the issues raised so far.

2 Using CBT to treat anxiety

→ What is cognitive behavioural therapy (CBT)?

CBT is a hands-on therapy that challenges the way we think in certain situations. Many people want to get some help with a situation but struggle to see how things can be different, and so the idea of change is hard for them to imagine. This book will explain how these changes can be made and give you an opportunity to try out these techniques in a way that is comfortable and doable for you.

When we break down the term 'cognitive behavioural therapy', we can see its main components:

▶ **Cognitive:** this part of CBT refers to our cognitions, or thoughts, and focuses on what we think in certain situations. CBT also focuses on our patterns of thinking and the way that our thoughts affect our anxiety and our behaviour.

▶ **Behavioural:** this part of CBT refers to our behaviour, or what we do, and again focuses on the way we behave in certain situations. CBT looks at the role that our behaviour plays in maintaining a particular problem or in affecting our mood.

▶ **Therapy:** this part of CBT refers to the changes we make using a variety of techniques and strategies. The emphasis here is on the word 'change'. CBT is a very practical and experiential therapy, whereby you try new ways of doing or thinking and monitor the impact of these changes.

> '*We are, perhaps, uniquely among the earth's creatures, the worrying animal. We worry away our lives.*'
>
> Lewis Thomas

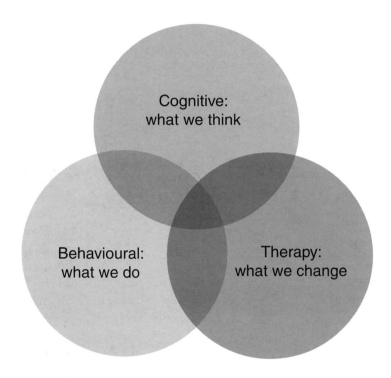

Previous therapies such as cognitive therapy (Beck, 1976) and behavioural therapy (Wolpe, 1958) have focused solely on one area, such as thoughts or behaviour, in isolation. However, CBT is based on the belief that many different factors, including our thoughts and behaviour, interact with, and impact on, each other in different ways in different situations. The following section describing the basic underpinnings of CBT explores this idea further.

THE UNDERPINNINGS OF CBT

CBT does not just focus on one area but instead it looks at the interactions between many different components. The premise of CBT is that our thoughts, feelings, behaviours and physical symptoms, together with the situation within which they occur, all affect and interact with each other. This is demonstrated in the 'five-areas' diagram below, which is often referred to as the 'hot cross bun' model (Padesky & Mooney, 1990) due to its appearance and the four different segments.

Situation:_____

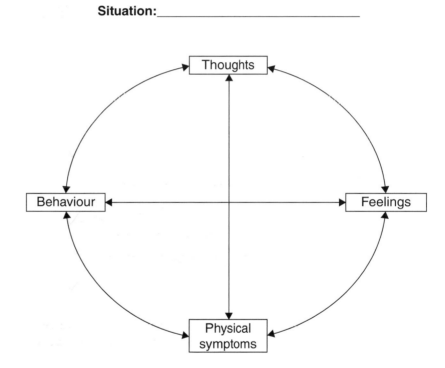

Exercise 5

LOOKING AT RESPONSES TO ANXIETY

Read the following example of the way the different components of anxiety can affect and interact with one another in a given situation.

Situation	Wake up and start worrying about the day ahead
Physical symptoms	Feel sick, heart rate increases, sweaty palms, tight chest
Thoughts	'I can't cope with today', 'I'm too anxious', 'I want to stay in bed.'
Behaviour	Try to ignore the anxiety and get out of bed
Feelings	Stressed, panicky and distracted; unable to focus on tasks; miserable

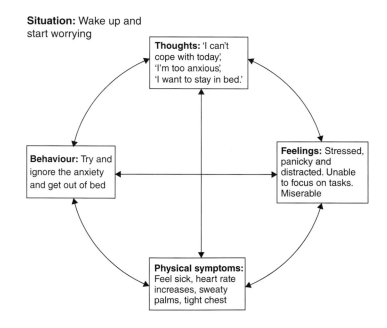

Situation: Wake up and start worrying

Thoughts: 'I can't cope with today', 'I'm too anxious', 'I want to stay in bed.'

Feelings: Stressed, panicky and distracted. Unable to focus on tasks. Miserable

Behaviour: Try and ignore the anxiety and get out of bed

Physical symptoms: Feel sick, heart rate increases, sweaty palms, tight chest

This example shows how physical symptoms can impact on our thoughts, feelings and behaviour.

Now think of a situation of your own that causes you anxiety and write down your reactions to it:

➜ Situation:

Worry that I'll have a heart attack.

→ Physical symptoms:

heart races, feel lightheaded, chest pain, sweating

→ Thoughts:

what if I die and leave my family, very afraid.

→ Behaviour:

try to go about day. often break down.

→ Feelings:

panicked, very scared, tired, hopeless.

. . . .

We can now begin to see how thinking differently about something might change our behaviour and subsequently our feelings. For example, see the diagram below.

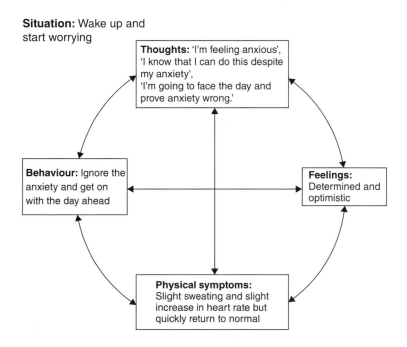

Situation: Wake up and start worrying

Thoughts: 'I'm feeling anxious', 'I know that I can do this despite my anxiety', 'I'm going to face the day and prove anxiety wrong.'

Behaviour: Ignore the anxiety and get on with the day ahead

Feelings: Determined and optimistic

Physical symptoms: Slight sweating and slight increase in heart rate but quickly return to normal

A basic principle of CBT is that, because all these areas interact with each other, we are able to change any one of these areas and see resulting changes in all aspects of a situation.

This is helpful because people may find it much easier to access one area than another. For example, in a particular situation we may be more aware of our physical symptoms than our thoughts, or more aware of how we feel than our behaviour. As one small shift can cause change in all these interlinked areas, it is also easy to see results and this helps us to build momentum to make other necessary changes.

If we believe in every situation that our thoughts, feelings, behaviour and physical symptoms all interact with one another and with the situation itself, then in order to see change we need to become aware of how we think, feel and act in a situation and then tackle one of these areas.

WHAT CAN CBT DO AND HOW DOES IT WORK?

In recent years CBT has received a lot of positive press, and for good reason. There is a strong evidence base that supports its principles and which shows impressive results for individuals who undergo the therapy.

CBT involves teaching individuals a number of different strategies to manage situations that they find challenging or difficult in some way. The aim of CBT is to help individuals to help themselves; in other words, the individual becomes equipped with the necessary skills and then becomes a kind of 'self-therapist'.

This is beneficial for several reasons:

1 By learning the skills and being able to put them into practice, you are able to increase your confidence in your ability to cope and deal with your anxiety.

2 Once learned, you have these skills for life and are not dependent on a therapist, or being in therapy, for ever.

3 The principles work for all areas of life, whether you are trying to face a particular problem or situation or just living your daily life.

4 CBT techniques inspire confidence and courage, meaning you'll feel better in yourself and notice an increase in your self-esteem.

CBT has been shown to be effective in treating many different types of disorder, from eating disorders to psychosis. However, CBT has been proven to be most effective in the treatment of anxiety disorders, such as panic disorder, obsessive–compulsive disorder and agoraphobia, and in the treatment of more general worry, depression and low mood.

I don't have a specific problem – will CBT still be useful?

▶ Every individual will experience at least one episode of low mood or anxiety in their lifetime, and most of us will experience several, not just as a result of major life events but also the stresses and strains of daily living. Therefore it is good to learn and apply CBT techniques to help reduce symptoms of anxiety, worry and low mood. CBT techniques can benefit everyone in some way, even if you don't feel you have a specific problem to address.

▶ CBT can be used to help build confidence, happiness, self-esteem and courage – all traits that could use a 'boost' from time to time.

HOW CAN SELF-HELP CBT HELP?

Since CBT aims to teach individuals strategies and skills so that they can become their own 'therapist' for life, they gain portable skills that they can carry into many differing situations and problems. In this way, self-help CBT can be extremely useful. You can learn and practise the skills being taught and see for yourself when they are helpful and work for you.

DO I NEED TO SEE A THERAPIST?

This book is in no way designed to be a replacement for one-to-one individual therapy. There are pros and cons of every therapy approach and, after reading this book, you may feel that you need extra support and would like to find a therapist. (If so, see the list of charity contacts and support numbers at the back of this book.)

If you have been suffering with low mood for some time, it is common to feel a lack of motivation, and sometimes a one-to-one therapist can provide support and encouragement to help you complete the CBT exercises. If you don't like the idea of seeing a therapist or are unsure about what this would entail, then this book will give you a good head-start by introducing you to the basic elements of CBT and some of the key strategies that you would cover in one-to-one CBT therapy. Ultimately, CBT is a very self-driven therapy, and self-help materials, such as this book, have been proven to be tremendously helpful (Williams, 2001).

However, if you feel very low or depressed, or feel that you need extra support in some way, contact your GP and arrange an appointment to discuss therapy options.

Never wait to tell people how you are feeling

It is far better and safer to tell those around you and be open and honest with your GP about your feelings and what you are struggling with. Your GP will want to help you and will be able to refer you directly for extra support, if this is what you feel you need.

The ultimate decision is yours, but whether you opt for individual therapy or choose a self-help route, this book will assist you by introducing you to CBT principles and teaching you valuable skills that you can apply in anxious situations.

→ Myths around CBT

Many myths surround CBT and the techniques involved. These can lead to doubts about the effectiveness of CBT as a therapy. CBT *is* a very effective and popular therapy and a good CBT approach would be to 'try it and see' rather than make up your mind first (but more of that later).

▶ **Myth 1**: CBT doesn't focus on the cause of the problem, only on the symptoms.

CBT as a therapy does not ignore the cause of the problem. The formulation process, which is when the therapist and individual map out what has led to the development of the problem, starts by looking at early experiences and 'critical incidents'. Critical incidents are the incidents or events that originally triggered the way we are feeling now, and in that sense CBT places a strong emphasis on the history, cause and development of a problem.

However, one of the most common phrases heard in therapy is 'I don't know why I feel like this, I just do'. For this reason, CBT does not get 'stuck' if there is no obvious history or apparent cause. Instead, CBT is able to start work on what is causing the most difficulty, e.g. feeling anxious or depressed, or being unable to leave the house, without needing first to focus on the history of the problem. In other words, CBT can treat the symptoms without needing to know the cause, although by no means is this cause ignored.

Symptoms first!

- A colleague of mine describes this idea wonderfully using the following example. He says, 'Imagine you broke your leg and received a bump to the head. When you get to the hospital and they ask you what happened, you say, 'I can't remember.' Wouldn't you want them to get on and treat your leg? Think how much pain you would be in and the damage you would do walking around on a broken leg, while waiting to remember the reason why it's broken! In this way, CBT works by fixing the leg first and then addressing the issue of how it became broken, in order to stop it happening again.'

- In the same way, CBT addresses the symptoms first, but it does not ignore the history or development of a problem.

▶ **Myth 2**: My anxiety comes and goes – CBT won't be useful for me.

Anxiety symptoms fluctuate and it may be that at the moment you feel well enough not to need therapy. One does not need to be experiencing a specific issue or problem at the time of therapy: you may have a situation which you would like to feel more confident about in the future, or you may like to increase your self-esteem. This book will give you an overview of the therapy and a chance to learn and develop some CBT for anxiety skills, which will be useful in a wide variety of future situations. In an anxiety-provoking situation, you will know how to face and overcome that anxiety.

▶ **Myth 3**: CBT is just common sense, surely? I don't need any more of that!

It is true that CBT is a logical and straightforward therapy, which is what makes it so accessible for so many people. However, when we are dealing with our thoughts and our emotions, we are often unable to apply a 'common sense' approach. Imagine, for example, that you are scared of spiders. If you came across one in your bathtub, do you think you would be able to think calmly and rationally in that moment? Probably not! CBT aims to give people strategies and techniques to apply a logical and balanced process to situations, which is difficult to achieve on our own without some form of input or support. What may sound simple on paper can actually be very challenging to put into practice.

Summary

1 CBT is proven to have great success in treating anxiety.

2 CBT works by teaching you the skills and techniques that, once learned, you can use in many different situations.

3 Although it is a logical approach, it is a lot more than 'just common sense'.

What I have learned

→ What are my thoughts, feelings and insights on what I have read so far?

_____

_____

_____

Use the space below to summarize any actions you identify as a result of reading this chapter.

_____

_____

_____

_____

Where to next?

This chapter will have given you an outline of CBT for anxiety and how and when it can be used. The next chapter discusses how to get started on this process. It looks at identifying common symptoms of anxiety and depression, and it will help you focus on your own situation.

3 Setting your goals and outcomes

....

In this chapter you will learn:

▶ why setting the right goals for therapy is essential in order to achieve success
▶ about the SMART goal-setting technique
▶ how to set your own SMART goals in order to overcome your anxiety.

....

→ What is a goal?

When we talk about 'goals', we are talking about something we want to attain or achieve in the future. This can be something in the near future, e.g. 'By the end of today I want to have completed this chapter,' or more long term, e.g. 'By the end of the year I want to have moved house.' Goals give us focus and something to aim for.

When used properly, goals can be motivating and encouraging, and can help us achieve whatever we want to achieve on a regular basis. Goals can also be used to bring about the change in our thoughts, feelings and behaviour that we are looking at throughout this book, and so it is important to get them right. This chapter is designed to help you set some goals that CBT techniques can then help you achieve.

> *'The greatest mistake you can make in life is to be continually fearing you will make one.'*
>
> Elbert Hubbard

→ Setting realistic goals

When they start therapy, many people I work with tell me that they 'just want to stop worrying'. Often, the picture they have of themselves anxiety free is never to have another anxious thought ever again. Unfortunately, this is not a realistic goal. Our thoughts naturally respond to life events and situations and it is impossible to predict the future in order to promise that nothing is going to happen to cause us anxiety.

However, the techniques and strategies in this book will teach you how to prevent fear and anxiety from becoming overwhelming. You can apply the techniques to stop anxiety preventing you from achieving wider goals. Have you hankered after that promotion, but worried you weren't good enough? Wanted to start a family but worried that you wouldn't cope? These are just a couple of the ways in which anxiety can prevent us from following what it is that we dream about or want to achieve.

By setting realistic goals for ourselves, without the boundaries and complications of anxiety, and without letting anxiety dictate what we can and can't achieve, we can begin to monitor progress and work towards a happier, anxiety-free future. Therefore, when setting goals, we cannot wish that nothing will ever make us anxious again, because that isn't a goal – it is just an unrealistic wish. However, we can work towards not being overwhelmed, being able to cope with situations and being able to move forward despite any anxiety.

By setting goals for therapy we are committing ourselves to overcoming anxiety and not letting it dictate our future. We work towards taking back control of our lives and breaking free from anxiety. We don't need an anxiety-free future, because we can learn how to handle anxiety instead. Anxiety won't go away but we can challenge it and face it and prevent it having a distressing or overwhelming impact on us and on our future. We can overcome our anxiety – and setting goals is the first step in deciding what your future looks like.

→ Recognizing success

One of the most common difficulties that anxiety presents is that anxiety is our worst critic. As soon as we achieve or accomplish anything, anxiety is waiting to say, 'Yes, but...' to us. 'Yes, but you didn't do it very well...' 'Yes, but you didn't finish it...' 'Yes, but you didn't do it quickly enough...' The reason anxiety answers us back in this way is because it needs us to have low self-esteem and a lack of confidence in ourselves – this way we are easier to bully.

Have you ever noticed how, on a day when you feel confident and happy, your anxiety can disappear, even if only temporarily? That isn't a coincidence. When we feel happy and strong, we are able to recognize our anxieties and dismiss them more easily.

One of the many reasons people fail to recognize their success in achieving their goals is because they constantly look ahead at how far they have to go, as opposed to reminding themselves of how far they've come. It is important to realize that anxiety works this way; it will stop us by telling us we are not good enough in the future. Remember, anxiety is a bully and a liar – do not trust it. Even one step in the right direction is one step further away from our anxiety, and it is a step that should be recognized and rewarded.

→ Working with goals

To some extent we work with goals every single day. We all have our own to-do lists, either carried round in our heads, scribbled on the back of an envelope or put into a diary on our smartphone. These may not sound like goals; after all, these are just the everyday things that we have to do. For example, on a typical to-do list we may have:

- ▶ Get food shopping
- ▶ Pay gas bill
- ▶ Post birthday card to friend

These may not sound like goals, but essentially they create a list of things that we want to achieve by the end of the day. The goals we set and carry around with us can affect our mood and our sense of achievement. Therefore it is important that the goals we hold for ourselves are meaningful and helpful, and that the goals we set for therapy are working towards a positive change or experience.

WHY ARE GOALS SO POWERFUL?

Have you ever set yourself some New Year's resolutions? It can be quite an exciting process. As you sit there making your list, you begin to picture an exciting and different future, and often a different 'you' as well. This will be the year you stop smoking/lose weight/get a new job/ stop drinking alcohol.

We can feel really motivated and encouraged at the thought of a better, brighter future. However, when at ten minutes past midnight we are standing there with a cigarette in one hand and a glass of wine in the other, we can feel as though we have failed already – with resolutions we made only ten minutes ago!

This immediate impact on mood may not matter on New Year's Eve after a night of celebrations but, over time, if we feel we are continually 'failing' to meet our goals, this can leave us feeling as though *we* are the failures. Feeling this way is very demotivating and can make us feel further away than ever from achieving what is important to us.

 When people tell me they cannot achieve their goals, it is usually a given that there is something wrong with the goal that has been set and not with the person who is trying to achieve it.

Setting goals is not as easy as just writing down or making a mental note of something you would like to do. That gets us nowhere (as countless broken New Year's resolutions have shown us). Instead, we need to focus on the right type of goal in order to make it achievable. There is no limit on what you can achieve; it just needs to be approached in the right way.

Exercise 6

LOOKING AT GOALS AND 'WISH LISTS'

The main difference between a list of goals and a 'wish list' tends to be how much control you have over achieving what's on the list. To try this out, write your top five items for a wish list here.

→ **My wish list** (e.g. win the Lottery)

1 _____

2 _____

3 _____

4 _____

5 _____

As you look at your wish list, ask yourself whether you have any control over these. If the answer if no or very little, then these are likely to be wishes rather than goals. Everyone has items on a wish list to some extent, but we cannot rely on making these wishes a reality because we have no control over them.

Goals, on the other hand, are a good way of getting results and the right goal helps to motivate us as well as achieve what we want.

→ Making my goals SMART

When we set our goals, they need to follow the SMART principle (Doran, 1981). The SMART principle breaks vague or broad goals down into specific, manageable tasks, by getting you to think about the goal under different headings. For example, the goal 'stop worrying' is a goal but it is not a SMART goal. This is because SMART goals need to be:

▶ **S** Specific
▶ **M** Measurable
▶ **A** Attainable
▶ **R** Realistic
▶ **T** Time-limited.

To give you an example, let's turn the goal 'stop worrying' into a SMART goal:

Goal	Specific?	Measurable?	Attainable?	Realistic?	Time-limited?	SMART?
Goal 1: Stop worrying.	No. There are no details here to specify what you mean by worrying or how you know when you are worrying.	No. There are no details that say how this will be measured.	Unknown. There is no way of knowing whether this is attainable or not because it's too vague, and no plan is in place.	Who knows? This depends on what you mean by worrying and the details of this plan.	No time limit has been set and so this is not a time-limited goal.	X This is not a SMART goal.
Goal 2: I would like to drive to work without feeling sick with anxiety and worrying about the day ahead. I would like this to happen within a month.	Yes. The details are clear and specific.	Yes. This can be measured by whether or not the worries occur in the car on the way to work.	Yes. There are no obvious problems standing in the way of you achieving this goal.	Yes. This is a realistic goal because the time set aside is plenty to practise the techniques and this is an everyday occurrence.	Yes. There is a time limit in place of one month.	√ This is a SMART goal

Looking at the examples above, think of some goals that you have previously set but haven't been able to achieve. Do they look like Goal 1 or Goal 2? The likelihood is that they look like Goal 1. We tend to think only about the 'end goal' or the desired effect rather than the specifics. However, it is only when our goals are broken down and made more specific and follow the SMART principles that they move from being vague items on a wish list to specific and achievable goals.

It can be difficult to start thinking in terms of SMART goals, particularly if it is something that we are not used to doing. In order to start the process, try not to limit yourself: first, let's think of what you want to achieve and then we will turn these into SMART goals later.

ANXIETY HAS NO PLACE IN YOUR GOALS

As you start to think about your goals and hopes for the future, you may well hear anxiety piping up in the background, telling you that you won't be able to do it, that you won't cope with it or that you are being daft for even thinking of these things. Take a moment to recognize just how poisonous anxiety is and then kick it out of your goal setting. These are *your* goals. Anxiety would set you a goal of sitting alone in a room all day worrying in order to give it priority.

Anxiety doesn't want you to achieve things, because in doing so you will prove to yourself that you are bigger and stronger than your anxiety. So just notice anxiety kicking up and then picture yourself free from anxiety. If you were the happiest and most confident person you can imagine, then what would your goals be? Forget anxiety-based limitations: this is about you and your goals. What would *you* like to achieve?

 Exercise 7

 WHAT WOULD YOU LIKE TO ACHIEVE?

Take a moment to picture yourself at your most confident and worry free. What would you like to achieve out of life if your anxiety didn't pose any problems for you? If it is hard to picture yourself anxiety free, talk to a friend, partner or family member. Note your ideas in the space below.

_____

_____

_____

_____

Alternatively, picture the most confident person you know and consider what goals they might set themselves. Could you also set yourself some of these goals? Note your ideas in the space below.

_____

_____

_____

The important thing is that your goals are relevant and meaningful for you, as this will give you the motivation to go out and achieve them.

→ Phase 1 of the goal-setting process

Setting goals is all about recognizing what is important to you and what you would like to achieve or change. You need to start from somewhere and so, before setting your SMART goals, it is important to begin by thinking about what is important to you and what you would like to change.

Dream big dreams – and then make them a reality!

 *Exercise 8*

 ### DEFINING YOUR THOUGHTS AND DESIRES

To start the goal-setting process, use the table below to start categorizing your thoughts/desires/goals. At this stage do not worry if they seem unrealistic or if they have been something you have already tried and 'failed' at (remember: it was probably the goal, not you!).

Take some time to think carefully about what is really important to you and the difference you would like to see in your life. Make these as big or as little as you like – these are your ideas and there are no right or wrong answers.

Use the categories below to help you define your own thoughts and desires, ready for goal setting. Use the examples given to inspire you.

Things I like in my life and would like more of	Things I don't like in my life that I would like to change	Values that are important to me as a person	People I would like a different relationship with	Things I would like to change about myself	Where I would like to be in five years
Spending time with my friends	I don't like feeling lonely.	Helping others	My colleagues – I've struggled to get to know them	I'd like to stop worrying so much and keep relaxed and happy when out.	I'd like to be in a fabulous new job with lots of colleagues and friends around me. I'd like to be relaxed and enjoy life more without worrying all the time.

→ Things I like in my life and would like more of:

_____

→ Things I don't like in my life that I would like to change:

_____

→ Values that are important to me as a person:

_____

→ People I would like a different relationship with:

_____

→ Things I would like to change about myself:

_____

→ Where I would like to be in five years:

_____

 **Exercise 9**

 ## SETTING SMART GOALS

In the previous exercise you may already have identified some goals or areas in your life/home/mood that you would like to improve on. For example, if you want to worry less about others, write that down.

Make a list of your initial goals here:

1 _____

_____

2 _____

_____

3 _____

_____

4 _____

_____

Looking at the SMART principles that we reviewed earlier, it is clear that the example given here is not a SMART goal and is therefore unlikely to be achieved.

Initial goal	Specific?	Measurable?	Attainable?	Realistic?	Time-limited?	SMART?
Worry less about others	No.	No.	No.	No.	No.	X – this is not a SMART goal.

Use the example in the table below as a template for working through your initial goals and turning them into SMART goals. The example shows the process of turning the goal 'worry less about others' into a SMART goal. Complete this table for your own goals, turning your initial goals into SMART goals.

Initial goal:	Specific?	Measurable?	Attainable?	Realistic?	Time-limited?	SMART?
e.g. Spend one hour every day when I'm not worrying about others. During this time I will bake and listen to the radio because I enjoy these activities and they relax me. I will do this when the children are at school so I won't be disturbed.	Yes. There is a specific plan in place to have some worry-free time in the day.	Yes. I can measure the amount of time I have to myself when I am not worrying about others.	Yes. Initial problems, e.g. being disrupted by the children, have already been planned for.	Yes. This is a realistic goal and should be relatively easy to fit into everyday life.	Yes. There is a time limit in place of one hour every day.	√ This is a SMART goal.

Initial goal:	Specific?	Measurable?	Attainable?	Realistic?	Time-limited?	SMART?

Once you have completed the table above, you should have a list of SMART goals that you can start working towards right away. Some of the goals you have set may be to do with your mood and how you are feeling, and you will be able to start working towards and completing those goals while working your way through this book. (Appendix 1 has a blank worksheet you can use for further goal setting.)

As everyone's goals are individual, this book is not geared towards specific goals. However, the strategies you will learn will focus on reducing anxiety. This in turn will leave you feeling more confident and with more energy to focus on yourself and your goals.

Summary

1　There is no limit to what you can achieve; only your anxiety will try and impose limits on you. You need to kick anxiety out of your goal setting in order to achieve what you want.

2　It is only when our goals are broken down and made more specific, following SMART principles, that they move from being vague items on a wish list to specific and achievable goals.

3　If you have tried and failed to achieve a goal previously, there is most likely something wrong with the goal, not with you. Go back to those goals and recreate them using the SMART techniques.

4　Remember not to let anxiety hold you back. Anxiety is a bully and a liar that will tell you that you cannot achieve. Let's start proving it wrong!

What I have learned

→ What are my thoughts, feelings and insights on what I have read so far?

_____

_____

_____

Use the space below to summarize any actions you identify as a result of reading this chapter.

_____

_____

_____

_____

Where to next?

The next chapter will help you identify your particular anxiety (or anxieties) and the way that they are affecting you. We will also look at unhelpful thoughts, feelings and behaviour that are maintaining these anxieties, and help you recognize when these may be triggered.

4 *What does my anxiety look like?*

· ·

In this chapter you will learn:

▶ how to make sense of your anxiety from a CBT point of view

▶ to map out the process of your anxiety and the impact it has on you

▶ to identify some of the underlying or 'maintaining' factors which may be feeding your anxiety and keeping it strong.

· ·

→ We are more than our anxiety

You should now have identified some of the key physical symptoms and feelings that you experience when you are anxious. This chapter will help you understand how they occur so that you can start to challenge them and thus begin to overcome your anxieties.

The reason why it is so important to externalize your anxiety – that is, separate out your anxiety and anxious thoughts from yourself – is because otherwise anxiety presents itself as factual, as though all your worries and fears are true and will happen. One of the ways it does this is by presenting them as your own thoughts.

When we talk about separating out anxiety's thoughts, it really is as though anxiety is a separate bully that invades us and gives us horrible anxious thoughts and worries. The reason why these are separate from our own thoughts is because without anxiety we would think something completely different.

For example, if you were particularly worried and anxious and you hit a bump in the road, you are much more likely to catastrophize and think 'Oh, my word, I just hit something!' whereas without anxiety you are much more likely to think 'Pesky pothole,' and drive on. Anxiety clouds our judgement and makes us instantly imagine the worst.

We will continue to think about the role of our anxiety in later chapters but, for now, let's just remember that we are *more* than our anxiety and therefore we have thoughts that are completely separate from our anxiety. We just need to find a way to recognize them.

> '*A hundredload of worry will not pay an ounce of debt.*'
>
> George Herbert

→ Building a picture of your anxiety

You have already identified the physical symptoms of your anxiety and where you felt them in your body. You also identified the key feelings you experienced alongside the anxiety. In order to complete the picture of your anxiety, we need to identify some of the other components, which include your trigger situations, thoughts and behaviour.

You may have several situations that make you feel anxious. If you feel constantly anxious, focus on situations where that anxiety is particularly bad and draw a picture of those situations. The process of bringing this out is to help you recognize the way in which your anxiety symptoms interact with one another and affect your thoughts, feelings, behaviour and physical symptoms.

This chapter is going to talk you through an example and show you how to draw out your anxiety. Once you have completed your drawing for one situation, you can draw out as many different situations as you like – there is a blank version of the cycle in Appendix 2, which you can copy and fill in as many times as you need.

Drawing out your anxiety in this way can help you identify why you are feeling anxious in situations that feel worrying or scary. Look at the following example before completing your own anxiety drawing in the next exercise.

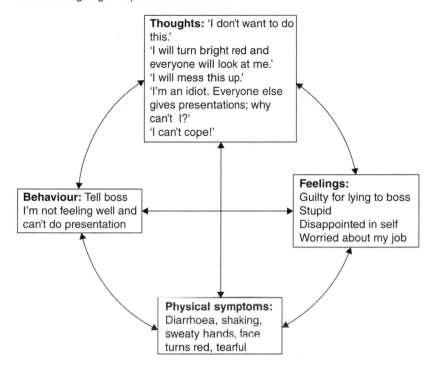

Situation that makes me feel anxious: Worrying about having to give a presentation at work

Thoughts: 'I don't want to do this.'
'I will turn bright red and everyone will look at me.'
'I will mess this up.'
'I'm an idiot. Everyone else gives presentations; why can't I?'
'I can't cope!'

Feelings:
Guilty for lying to boss
Stupid
Disappointed in self
Worried about my job

Behaviour: Tell boss I'm not feeling well and can't do presentation

Physical symptoms: Diarrhoea, shaking, sweaty hands, face turns red, tearful

This person may not have the same thoughts, feelings, behaviour and physical symptoms in every situation. Other situations that they cannot avoid or get out of may also cause them anxiety but lead to very different reactions for them. However, you can see from this example of having to give a presentation at work how anxiety can affect every aspect of a situation, with a knock-on effect on the next part of this cycle.

You can also see how many different elements interact with one another. For example, the thought 'I will mess this up' may increase this person's feelings of stupidity and worry about their job. Knowing that all these elements interact and affect each other means that you can work out your own anxiety picture by looking at how the elements interact with each other in your own anxiety situation.

DRAWING YOUR OWN ANXIETY PICTURE

Start by recognizing an anxiety-provoking situation you experience.

→ Situation:

_____

_____

Now list all the different thoughts, feelings, behaviours and physical symptoms that you experience in this situation.

→ Thoughts: In this situation I think:

_____

_____

→ Feelings: In this situation I feel:

_____

_____

→ Physical symptoms: In this situation I experience the following physical symptoms:

_____

_____

→ Behaviour: When I'm in this situation, I do the following:

_____

_____

Next, plot these out on the following blank diagram to show how they are interacting with each other.

Situation that makes me feel anxious:_____

_____

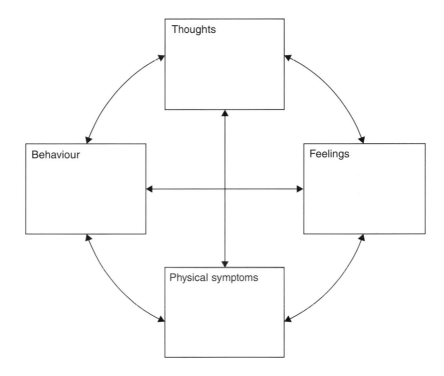

Use the drawing above to focus on and recognize what you actually *do* when you are anxious.

The reason why focusing on behaviour is so important is because what you do when you are in an anxiety-provoking situation will affect how you feel after that situation is over.

→ # Looking at our behaviour when anxious

As we have seen in the examples above, what we do impacts on our thoughts and how we feel as well as our physical symptoms, and so our behaviour influences the other elements of a particular situation.

Two types of behaviour are very common in individuals with anxiety. They are:

▶ avoidance

▶ safety behaviour.

Exercise 11

AM I AVOIDING?

Look at the table below and tick any of the items that you feel apply to you.

Behaviour	Tick
I will make an excuse to get out of a situation.	
I will pretend to be ill or say I am too tired to do something, even if that isn't true.	
I will ask someone else to do something for me rather than do it myself.	
I will not answer the door and will ignore my phone.	
I won't open letters or bills .	
I will make sure someone else is responsible for the last action, e.g. let my partner close and lock the door/put the children to bed or let a colleague lock up at work.	
I will bite my tongue and not say anything even if someone is wrong.	
I will fill my time completely so that I cannot do a particular activity.	
When I have to do something, I will get out of the situation as quickly as possible.	
As soon as I feel anxious in a situation. I will make an excuse and leave.	

If you have ticked any of the behaviour listed above, you are avoiding. This is not an exhaustive list and you may be avoiding in other ways as well.

→ Does it matter if I avoid?

Yes! On the surface, avoidance may not seem to be doing any harm. It is common to start to avoid situations when we feel uncomfortable about them or unable to cope with them in some way. Often with anxiety, we will avoid situations because we simply don't think we'll cope with, or want to deal with, the anxiety that we think will arise as a consequence. However, if we continually avoid situations, we may become socially isolated very quickly which, in turn, can have a drastic impact on our mood.

The more we avoid a situation, the harder it becomes to face that situation because it then becomes a much bigger deal. For example, if you avoided housework for a year, your house would be much harder to clean and the task would feel more overwhelming than if you faced doing a little bit every day.

The same is true with anxiety. If you continue to avoid doing something, it can feel as though the pressure is mounting, and pretty soon that situation or task is going to feel too big to tackle and too difficult to cope with, and then we reach a point where we *cannot* do something, even if we want or need to.

THE 'ACCIDENTAL AVOIDER'

Have you ever noticed how, when you want to avoid a situation, suddenly tackling the sock drawer becomes more pressing? Sometimes we may unconsciously avoid something and not realize that we are distracting ourselves from thinking about or doing something that we don't want to focus on. We may also avoid situations that may make us feel anxious or that we are not sure we can cope with, without realizing we are doing so. This is what I call 'accidental avoidance' and often people do not realize they are doing it.

It is important to recognize, however, that all this avoidance doesn't mean anxious people are lazy – far from it! In fact, anxious people are often extremely busy, filling their days with distracting activities and work, and often finding it difficult to sit still. Most people with anxiety will tell me that they struggle to relax, that they are unable to sit and watch a film, and their friends and family will describe them as 'always on the go'. This is because, when they stop being busy, anxious people can become overwhelmed with anxious thoughts. Keeping busy feels a far safer option.

WHY DOES AVOIDANCE MATTER?

Avoidance can feel as though it is preventing you from becoming anxious. However, what very few people realize is that avoidance actually *maintains* anxiety. This is because, by avoiding certain situations, we never get an opportunity to disconfirm the beliefs we hold about that situation. Continually avoiding means that we never gather any evidence for or against that belief and so we continue to hold on to the unhelpful belief.

As long as you keep avoiding, you're never challenging anxiety and therefore never proving it wrong. So, while avoidance can feel helpful at keeping your anxiety at bay, it is in fact maintaining anxiety and acts as anxiety's best friend.

THE MAINTENANCE CYCLE OF AVOIDANCE

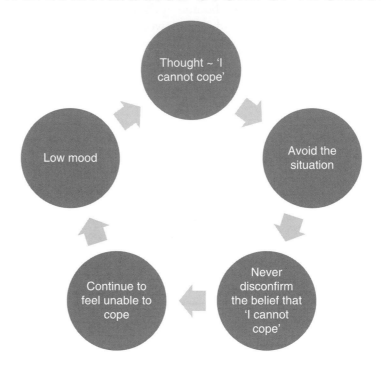

Every time you avoid something, you are adding a little bit of strength to the idea that your anxiety and your anxious thought are right. Because of this, the longer you avoid, the harder it can then feel to face a difficult or challenging situation, as anxiety will have been greatly strengthened before you challenge this.

→ The anxiety peak

It is important to understand how anxiety works and what it looks like. If you feel anxious, it is a common experience to feel as though your anxiety is going up and up and may never stop, and so we picture our anxiety continuing for ever, as shown in this graph.

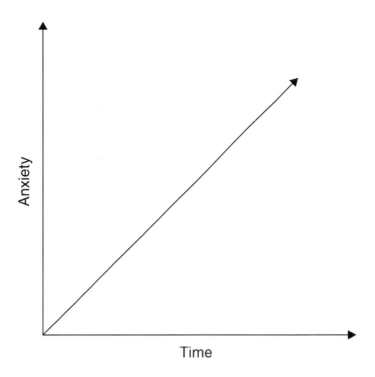

When we avoid a situation, we cut that anxiety short as we escape the situation that is making us anxious – and so our anxiety is immediately reduced, as shown here.

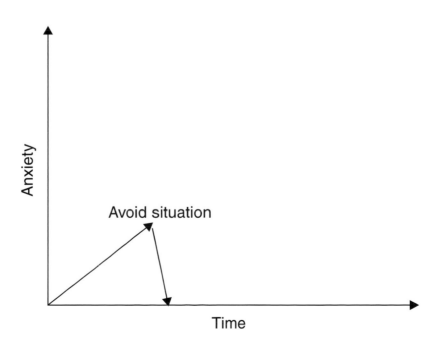

However, this anxiety is only temporarily reduced. Avoiding the situation makes it much harder to go back into another time: avoiding makes us lose confidence in ourselves and so the anxiety comes back stronger every time. This means that we can experience anxiety in ever-increasing peaks and avoidance may not be as effective at reducing our anxiety, as shown here.

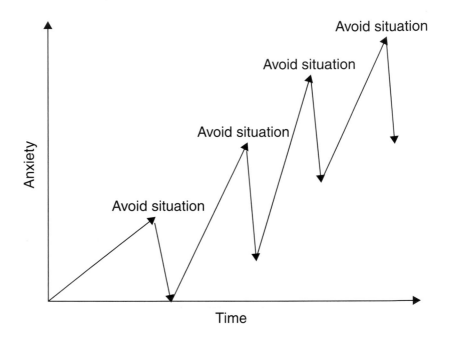

As you can see from the diagram above, although the anxiety is reduced, this reduction is temporary and the initial anxiety levels keep increasing.

PLOTTING YOUR ANXIETY GRAPH

Think of a situation that makes you anxious that you have recently avoided or escaped. Plot your own anxiety graph below. What does your anxiety look like in this situation?

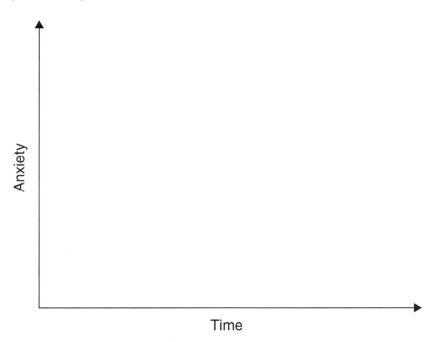

We tend to avoid and escape situations as soon as we feel anxious. However, anxiety does not continue increasing indefinitely. Our bodies are designed to limit and reduce anxiety naturally over a period of about 20–25 minutes. This means that, when we feel anxious, if we stay in the situation rather than immediately escape and avoid it, our anxiety would naturally reduce and we would feel less anxious.

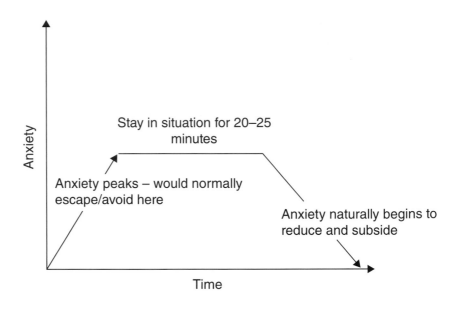

As you can see from the graph above, our anxiety cannot continue to increase for ever. Instead, once anxiety peaks, if we are able to tolerate a situation for 20–25 minutes, our anxiety will start to reduce and will gradually disappear. This is a more challenging experience because escape and avoidance provide us with immediate and rapid relief from our anxiety symptoms, whereas by staying in the situation we have to tolerate our own symptoms of anxiety for a time before they begin to subside.

However, by staying in the experience, we discover that we can handle difficult and anxiety-provoking situations without the need to avoid them, which means we can do so much more than if we are constantly having to escape. Discovering that you can cope with a situation that you previously thought you couldn't is wonderful for your confidence and self-esteem. We will be looking at how you stay in those situations later in the book.

It's never too late

It's never too late to start challenging and overcoming your anxiety. We will look at the approach to challenging your avoidance in more detail in a later chapter. For now, rest assured that you can always tackle your anxiety, at any age and at any stage, no matter how long you have been using avoidance or safety behaviour.

→ Safety behaviour

Safety behaviour is the range of things we do or have with us that make us feel safe or more in control of our anxiety. Safety behaviour can take many forms; avoidance is just one example of safety behaviour.

WHAT'S MY SAFETY BEHAVIOUR?

Look at the different types of safety behaviour listed below and identify the ones that apply to you. Complete the details of your own safety behaviour in the empty column to help you identify which ones you currently engage in.

Common safety behaviour	Detail of my safety behaviour
Carrying something with me, e.g. a bottle of water, mints or a paper bag, to help me calm down when I feel anxious	
Removing all distractions, e.g. turning the radio off or silencing conversations while doing something that feels important, in case it distracts me and I get it wrong	
Asking my partner/friend/colleague to do something for me, so I don't have to do it	
Avoiding touching something that I think is dangerous	
Only travelling on routes I know, in case I get lost and cannot get home	

Common safety behaviour	Detail of my safety behaviour
Arriving everywhere very early	
Asking other people to check things for me/check that I have done something properly	
Repeating actions/tasks to check they are done properly	
Immediately stopping an activity if I feel anxious, in case it affects my health	
Avoiding things I used to enjoy doing because I don't think they are good for me any more, e.g. exercise, socializing	
Doing everything in a set routine	
Counting while doing something/engaging in an activity	

Now list here any other behaviour or things that you carry or do that make you feel safe when in an anxiety-provoking situation. These may be superstitious things or everyday things that make you feel safer or less anxious.

1 _____

_____

2 _____

_____

3 _____

_____

4 _____

_____

5 _____

_____

Looking at the safety behaviours you have identified above, consider the role they play. What is it about these that keeps you safe? Here is an example to help you.

My safety behaviour	*Carrying a bottle of water with me*
How does this help me?	*When I am anxious, my mouth goes dry and I find it hard to swallow and I feel as though I will choke. Carrying the water helps me as it makes it easier for me to swallow and makes me less likely to choke.*

Now consider your own safety behaviour and complete the table below (continue on to additional paper if necessary).

My safety behaviour	
How does this help me?	
My safety behaviour	
How does this help me?	
My safety behaviour	
How does this help me?	
My safety behaviour	
How does this help me?	
My safety behaviour	
How does this help me?	

At this stage you don't need to do anything further. However, we will come back to some of this safety behaviour later, so keep your list somewhere handy so that you can review it over a few chapters.

Summary

1 Avoidance is a safety behaviour that actually maintains our anxiety and makes it worse.

2 All the elements of an anxiety-provoking situation interact and affect one another. It is important to work out your own anxiety picture and how these elements interact in your own situation.

3 It's never too late to start challenging and overcoming your anxiety.

What I have learned

→ What are my thoughts, feelings and insights on what I have read so far?

_____

_____

_____

Use the space below to summarize any actions you identify as a result of reading this introduction.

_____

_____

_____

_____

Where to next?

Having identified some of your anxious thoughts and behaviour, the next two chapters focus on how you can start to challenge and overcome your anxiety. First, we will examine the most effective ways to overcome your anxious thinking.

5 Challenge to change: overcoming anxious thinking

In this chapter you will learn:

▶ how to monitor and record your anxious thoughts so that you can start to identify your thought patterns and 'thinking errors'

▶ why certain thoughts that occur in particular situations cause you anxiety

▶ how to challenge and overcome these thoughts so that they diminish in strength and become less frequent.

In previous chapters you have been able to identify the physical and emotional impact that anxiety has on your body. This has allowed you to tune into the anxiety and the effect that it has on you. This is a very important part of recognizing when you are anxious. Now we are going to focus on the anxious thoughts that occur in particular situations and gain some understanding of why these thoughts are causing you anxiety.

Once we are aware of the thoughts we are having in particular situations, we can start challenging these thoughts so that they will begin to lose their power and become less frequent. This means that you will be able to relax and enjoy yourself, without anxious thoughts, in situations that previously made you anxious.

> *'There are very few monsters who warrant the fear we have of them.'*
>
> André Gide

→ Monitoring your anxiety

In order to understand them, you first need to monitor the anxious thoughts you are having and write them down using a 'thought record sheet'. The thought record sheet should be completed either during or as soon after an anxious situation as possible, to allow for accurate monitoring.

The following thought record sheet is a guide to what you need to record, but you may find a different way more helpful or convenient. Many people copy the headings across into a document on their laptop or smartphone so that they can complete the thought record discreetly. How you decide to complete it is up to you; the main thing is to record the information somewhere so that you can review it and refer back to it.

Advance warning

When people start to monitor their anxious thinking, they often feel as though they are having more thoughts as a result and they worry about making their anxiety worse. This won't happen, though. The reason you may feel as if you are experiencing more anxious thoughts is because you are focusing your attention on the thoughts, rather than trying to ignore them or distracting yourself away from them. Therefore, when we start to focus on these thoughts, we become aware of just how many thoughts we are having at any given time and this can be more than we were expecting.

Exercise 14

COMPLETING YOUR THOUGHT RECORD

The thought record below has five columns to be completed. You are already skilled at identifying the physical symptoms and emotions of your anxiety. We are adding to these skills by building the full picture of your anxiety, including the situation, the thoughts or worries that went through your mind, and your behaviour, i.e. what you did in that situation.

Here is an example of a thought record to help you:

Situation	Thoughts	Feelings	Physical symptoms	Behaviour
About to give a presentation at work	'I can't do this.' 'I'm not good enough.' 'People will judge me and think I don't know what I'm talking about.'	Panic Wanting to escape Stress Anger with self	Sweaty palms Shaky Nausea	Told boss I had a migraine and could not do the presentation. Left the room and felt tearful and stressed. Eventually got my bag and went home for the rest of the day.

Now create and complete your own thought record for many different situations. Any way of doing this can be successful, so choose an option that suits you best, using the headings in the table.

Situation	Thoughts	Feelings	Physical symptoms	Behaviour
1				
2				
3				
etc.				

Some people monitor and record every situation for up to a week. This is the best way to do the recording because it allows for a broad overview of many different situations.

However, some people find constantly completing the records a bit daunting, in which case I would suggest completing the records for five or six stressful or anxiety-provoking situations, in as much detail and as close to the events themselves as you can. This will allow you to gain good insight into your thoughts during a highly anxious situation. Find a blank version of the record in Appendix 3.

Once you have completed the records, you can start to identify different thought patterns and search for 'thinking errors'. Thinking errors are very common in anxiety, as the anxiety skews how we interpret situations and these 'thinking errors' distort the way we think about ourselves and others, and about different situations.

Exercise 15

IDENTIFYING THINKING ERRORS

Read the list of common anxious-thinking errors below. Then go through your thought records to see whether you can identify any thinking errors. It may be helpful to get someone you trust to help you do this in order to get an objective opinion.

→ **1 Black-and-white thinking**

This is also known as 'all or nothing' thinking, whereby people tend to think in extremes. For example, a situation can either be brilliant or awful, people can either be lovely or horrible, we can think of ourselves as perfect or the worst person ever. With black-and-white thinking there is no grey area. Instead, we think in absolutes.

→ Your examples:

_____

_____

→ **2 Catastrophic thinking**

This is, as it sounds, thinking the worst or imagining a catastrophic outcome during seemingly everyday 'normal' experiences. This may mean that feeling unable to complete a presentation leads you to worry about losing your job, being unable to pay your bills and being evicted from your home. Catastrophic thinking tends to escalate quickly towards the worst-case scenario.

→ Your examples:

_____

_____

→ **3 Mind reading**

Mind reading refers to thoughts that predict others' responses or thoughts: 'People will think I'm an idiot', 'People will look at me', 'People will know I'm nervous.' When we mind read, we anticipate what other people's responses will be and find ourselves worrying or reacting to our predictions before an event takes place (e.g. not delivering a presentation because we have predicted that people will laugh at us).

➜ Your examples:

_____

_____

➜ **4 Disqualifying the positive**

This refers to the way we dismiss or belittle positive achievements or experiences and fail to recognize our own role in them. We may attribute any success to luck rather than our own hard work (e.g. 'I was lucky to get that promotion.') but we take the blame for negative events in our lives.

➜ Your examples:

_____

_____

➜ **5 Filtering**

When we see the world through a negative or anxious filter, we are unable to see the positive or good things that happen around us and we focus only on negative events or worries. For example, we may have been to a lovely dinner party and had a great time, but on the way home we realize that we left our umbrella there. This then becomes our entire focus so that, rather than thinking about the nice time we had and remembering our enjoyment, we think negatively about the whole evening and feel foolish and anxious.

➜ Your examples:

_____

_____

→ Am I allowed to worry about that?

In CBT we talk about being 'allowed' to think something or worry about something.

Consider the thinking errors that you have identified in the previous exercise. If any of your anxious thoughts fall into one of those categories, then you are not 'allowed' to be anxious about it. This is because the anxieties are not based on fact. Instead, you are basing your anxiety on the worries that anxiety is giving you in the first place.

If you are worried that people will laugh at you, you are not allowed to be anxious about that until you do something and people laugh at you. Up to that point, you have nothing to worry about or react to, as *nothing has happened*.

We can create whole scenarios and conversations in our head, thinking about what could go wrong or how someone would react to us, and all that energy and anxiety are being poured into a situation that doesn't actually exist. We need to overcome these anxieties by questioning our thoughts, scanning for thinking errors and looking for the evidence.

We need to remember that, unless we have concrete evidence for our anxieties, we are not allowed to worry about them.

CHALLENGING ANXIOUS THOUGHTS

Here are some typical anxious thoughts and the questions we can ask to challenge them.

- ▶ Thought: 'Everyone will laugh at me.'
- ▶ Challenge: How do you know? Have you asked 'everyone'? Who is 'everyone' anyway? How do you know they'll laugh at you? Even if they've laughed before, that's not proof that they will this time.
- ▶ Thought: 'I can't do this.'
- ▶ Challenge: Is that true or just an anxious thought? What's the worst that will happen if you attempt it? What if you can do it and these doubts are just anxious thoughts?
- ▶ Thought: 'I'm not good enough.'
- ▶ Challenge: Could this be low self-esteem rather than fact? What would make you feel good enough? If you don't do something because you don't feel good enough, isn't that just confirming your disappointment, rather than challenging the belief? There's no more evidence saying you are not good enough than there is saying that you are good enough, so why not try it?

Exercise 16

CHALLENGING ANXIOUS THINKING

You can see that we can begin to question and challenge our anxious thinking by recognizing the impact of our thinking errors and anxiety. Start questioning your anxiety from now on. Challenge it and stand up to it by looking for the concrete evidence for and against that thought.

Use the following table to record your anxious thoughts and the evidence for and against them.

Anxious thought	Evidence for the thought	Evidence against the thought

Sometimes we can be unsure of the outcome of a situation, which can make challenging harder – we simply don't *know* what an outcome will be. When this happens, we can use behavioural experiments to test out our anxious beliefs and help us gather evidence against them. Behavioural experiments will be examined in detail in the next chapter.

→ Breaking the anxiety habit

When we feel anxious, it can feel as though anxiety has a really tight grip on us and we are powerless to resist. When anxiety tells us to do something or worry about something, we respond immediately, trying to alleviate some of that feeling. In other words, anxiety says 'Jump!' and we say 'How high?'

In order to regain some control over our lives, we need to break the habit of responding so quickly to anxiety. We can do this by building in a buffer of 20–25 minutes before we respond. We have already looked at the pattern of anxiety peaks and seen how after 20–25 minutes our anxiety will naturally start to subside. This means that, if you wait before responding to your anxiety, the anxiety may go away without you having to do anything.

Even if the anxiety doesn't go completely, you are still breaking the habit so that you are no longer at anxiety's beck and call. For example, let's say I become anxious about whether I offended someone at work. My anxiety would be telling me, 'Oh, no! I must call them right away and apologize!' However, I want to break that instant-response habit, so instead I simply note the anxiety and then wait 20–25 minutes while doing something else, and then decide whether I actually need to call them or not. By that time the initial anxiety may have passed and I may have decided that I don't need to call them after all. If I do go ahead and decide to call them, I have had time to calm down and gather my thoughts, so that the phone call is much more likely to be useful and pleasant.

→ Anxiety and safety behaviour

As discussed in a previous chapter, safety behaviours are one of the most common strategies we use to help us manage all types of anxiety. They could involve doing something small – such as carrying a bottle of water or a packet of mints in case you feel anxious and your mouth feels dry – to something more extreme, such as not going anywhere without your 'safety person' with you. When we use people in our safety behavior – for example, not going shopping without our partner in case we have a panic attack – we think we need them there to look after us. By taking that person with you, they have effectively become your safety behaviour.

You may be thinking, 'What's wrong with safety behaviour?' The problem is that safety behaviour acts to reinforce or confirm our anxious thoughts, as in the following case study.

Alan's story

'When I get in the car with my child, I worry about someone crashing into the car and my child being hurt. I get very panicky when I'm in the car, my hands are sweaty and my heart beats too quickly. I worry that I will collapse at the wheel and would be unable to get help quickly enough to help my child and that whoever had hit us would drive away and not help.

'To stop this happening, I have developed a safety behaviour of dialling emergency services on my mobile but not hitting 'call'. I do this so that, if anything did happen, I could literally hit 'call' straight away and then help would come really quickly. I have started to hold the phone in my hand while driving so that I am ready to call the police and ambulance and I've started to memorize the number of the car behind me so that I could give that information to the police. I think having this system in place helps me and protects me and my daughter from being hurt.'

In this case study we can identify two safety behaviours:

▶ holding the mobile phone with the emergency number already dialled
▶ memorizing the number plates of other cars on the road.

It is easy to see that these safety behaviours are far from keeping Alan and his child safe. Let's consider the risk he is running by trying to memorize the number plates of the car behind him. His attention will not be focused on the road or on the other cars around him and he will constantly be distracted. This probably places him at more risk and makes it much more likely that he *will* have an accident, as his full and focused attention is not on the road. The fact that he is also holding a mobile phone and therefore cannot grip the steering wheel properly or use his hand quickly in an emergency places him at even higher risk.

These 'safety' behaviours are actually increasing the risk of these feared events happening. They could be relabelled 'danger behaviours'.

Exercise 17

IDENTIFYING YOUR SAFETY BEHAVIOUR

Think back to the last time you were feeling anxious or panicky and identify your own safety behaviour. Was there anything about that safety behaviour that could in fact have distracted you or made things worse? Note down your answers below.

→ My behaviour:

_____

→ How it made things worse:

_____

→ My behaviour:

_____

→ How it made things worse:

_____

→ My behaviour:

_____

→ How it made things worse:

_____

→ My behaviour:

_____

→ How it made things worse:

_____

→ The problem of safety behaviour

Safety behaviours are self-fulfilling in nature. That is, they provide false 'evidence' that means they become more believable and necessary to us. I'll give you an example. Let's say I believe that, if I check three times that my front door is locked, then I won't be burgled. This means that every time I leave the house I check three times that the front door is locked and every time I come home, I haven't been burgled. My anxiety tells me this is proof that I *need* to check my front door three times as this has stopped me from being burgled.

The act of checking the front door three times may seem a very small effort compared with the fear of being burgled and so I continue to check the front door. The problem with this is that I am now worrying about whether or not I checked the front door three times and get upset if I believe I have forgotten to check the door. Also, I never find out what happens if I *don't* check the front door. Will I be burgled if I just lock the door without checking it three times? I'll never know: it feels risky or 'dangerous' now not to check. This means I am now stuck in a cycle of carrying out my safety behaviour with no idea how to break out of it.

This may not seem problematic with a small or brief safety behaviour, but it is very likely that you may have more than one. These actions themselves then become something to feel anxious about and they cause more anxiety and panic. It is the same with the example above, where Alan is never testing whether he is safe to drive without having to pre-dial the emergency number and memorize the number plates of other cars. He is disconfirming his anxious beliefs.

 Exercise 18

 ## DITCHING YOUR SAFETY BEHAVIOUR

Take a moment to reconsider the range of safety behaviour you identified earlier. Consider some of the cycles you may be caught up in and things you would find very difficult to stop doing. Note them below.

1 _____

2 _____

3 _____

If you think you can't manage without a safety behaviour, gather some evidence to challenge it. Keep a record of the following.

→ What you thought would happen:

_____

→ What did happen:

_____

→ How you feel about that initial fear now:

_____

When you feel you have enough evidence to tell you a situation is safe, you will be able to ditch your safety behaviour.

You will then discover that situations *are* safe, that anxiety passes and that you can cope. In doing so, you will increase your confidence in your own ability to manage anxious situations and realize that you don't need any props or 'help' to get you through. You *can* do this – you just need to believe it.

There is more on the principles of behavioural experiments in Chapter 6.

Beware the hidden safety behaviour!

Driving a different route to work? Avoiding a phone call? Carrying something with you? Deliberately avoiding specific people, places or things? Beware the hidden safety behaviour. If you have been experiencing anxiety for a long time, it is likely that you have developed many different safety behaviours without realizing it. This may also mean that you haven't experienced anxiety for a long time.

For example, if avoiding somewhere that makes you anxious is your safety behaviour, you won't experience the anxiety. Sometimes we can confuse being well with avoiding everything that makes us anxious. You want to be able to face any situation free from fear, and not have to avoid certain people, places or situations. Take the challenge and face anxiety on your own – you will beat it and you'll feel a lot better and stronger for it.

Summary

1   Thinking errors are very common in anxiety, as the anxiety skews how we interpret situations. These 'thinking errors' distort the way we think about ourselves and others and about situations.

2   In order to regain some control over our own lives, we need to break the habit of responding so quickly to anxiety.

3   Safety behaviour may feel helpful to us but it reinforces and confirms our anxious thoughts, so that it makes our anxiety worse in the long term.

4   We need to ditch our safety behaviours to build our confidence and feel good about ourselves.

What I have learned

→ What are my thoughts, feelings and insights on what I have read so far?

_____

_____

_____

Use the space below to summarize any actions you identify as a result of reading this chapter.

_____

_____

_____

_____

Where to next?

This chapter has focused on challenging your anxious thoughts and seeking evidence for and against your anxious beliefs. The next chapter focuses on using behavioural experiments to help you test out some of your anxious beliefs and gather further evidence against them. What you thought would happen:

6 Using behavioural experiments to overcome anxious thoughts

• •

In this chapter you will learn:

▶ what behavioural experiments are and when to use them

▶ how they can help you overcome anxiety

▶ how to carry out behavioural experiments to reduce your anxiety.

• •

By the end of this chapter you will have completed a behavioural experiment that challenges an anxious thought. You will also be equipped with the knowledge and skills to continue doing further behavioural experiments to reduce your anxiety.

As the name suggests, a behavioural experiment is an experiment that involves an aspect of behaviour. When conducting a behavioural experiment, we try out or test our behaviour in a particular situation and then carefully monitor the results of this behaviour.

Behavioural experiments are important because they provide an element of evidence that is otherwise unattainable. Previously we discussed the idea of 'evidence' for thoughts and that in CBT *you are not allowed to think or feel something without strong evidence for that thought*. When we are feeling anxious, anxiety will frequently **tell** us something and we often accept this as fact.

> '*As a rule, what is out of sight disturbs men's minds more seriously than what they see.*'
>
> Julius Caesar

Exercise 19

THE 'FACTS' ANXIETY TELLS US

Here are some examples of 'facts' that anxiety may tell us. See how many you recognize:

→ You're not good enough.

→ You won't be able to cope.

→ You'll muck it up/get it wrong.

→ You can't do this.

Use the space below to write down some of the other 'facts' that anxiety tells you about yourself.

_____

_____

_____

_____

_____

_____

_____

_____

Now consider the 'facts' you have highlighted and review the evidence for these anxious thoughts. Do you have any concrete evidence? Remember, thinking errors and guessing do not count. Note down the evidence for your thoughts in the table below.

Thought	Evidence for	Evidence against	Am I allowed to worry about this? (Yes/No)

In some cases, when we try to find evidence for and against the thought that is causing us so much anxiety, we simply do not have any evidence – either for or against. This is usually due to avoidance or another unhelpful behaviour that has stopped us being in the situation to be able to gather any evidence against the thought.

→ Why behavioural experiments work

CBT says that you are not allowed to worry about something unless you have evidence that you should be worried about it. This means that, whenever we get anxious about something, we need more than fear or anxiety to justify our worry: we need *proof*. Behavioural experiments allow us to test out, in a controlled and contained fashion, any worries or beliefs we may hold. They make completing the task and gathering the evidence easier and less daunting.

A key component of behavioural experiments is that they target a specific thought or belief that you have. To help demonstrate this, let's look at the following case study.

Kayleigh's story

Kayleigh and her husband have recently moved to a new area. Kayleigh has been off paid work after giving birth to her daughter two years ago. She is keen to meet other mums so that her daughter can make friends and settle into nursery, but she worries that the other mums will snub her. She feels that the new area is posher and more upmarket than the old one, she thinks other mums will work and have careers, and that they will judge her for not working. Kayleigh also feels that, because she hasn't done much recently apart from move house and look after her daughter, she is dull and uninteresting.

At a nursery open day, she meets a small group of other mums who invite her to a coffee morning the following week. Kayleigh feels she should go but worries that she will stand out, be unable to think of anything interesting to say, and that the other mums will ask why she isn't back at work yet. Kayleigh also worries that the other mums will think she is wrong for the area and snub her when they get to know her. Kayleigh is considering not going.

Poor Kayleigh: a friendly invitation to a coffee morning has turned into an anxiety-fuelled nightmare for her, to the extent that she is considering not going despite the fact that she really wants and needs to make new friends. When Kayleigh considers her strongest worry about this situation, she says:

'I worry that other people will reject me. I won't be good enough for them and, when they get to know me, they won't like me and I'll be all alone in a new area.'

Kayleigh is engaging in a number of thinking errors such as 'mind reading' and 'predicting the future' and so she needs to set up a behavioural experiment to find out whether she is allowed to be anxious about this. Kayleigh rates her belief that the other mums will snub her at 100 per cent. However, she has no evidence for this belief.

Kayleigh conducts a behavioural experiment and goes to the coffee morning, expecting the people there either to take no interest in her or to reject her once they get to know her. She stays for the full three hours and leaves with many more invitations. She is made to feel welcome and that people are interested in her and her daughter. No one comments on her not working; several of the other women there have also not returned to work yet.

Kayleigh no longer believes that she is uninteresting or going to be rejected by these women. Her belief rating goes down to 0 per cent.

→ How behavioural experiments work

Behavioural experiments work by targeting a specific cognition and helping an individual find enough evidence for or against their thought in order to increase or reduce their belief in the thought. Had Kayleigh not completed this experiment by attending the coffee morning, she would have continued to carry around the belief that others would reject her, without any evidence to support this belief.

Behavioural experiments can be used not only to disprove negative beliefs and thoughts but also to gain evidence for positive beliefs.

SETTING UP A BEHAVIOURAL EXPERIMENT

There are three steps to setting up a behavioural experiment.

▶ **Step 1: Identify the 'key' cognition or belief to be tested**

The first step is to identify the specific thought or belief that you are going to test. To do this, you are going to need to use the thought record you completed previously to help you. Review the thought record and identify the key anxieties that occurred. Patterns of worry may be tied to specific situations, e.g. being at work or with other people, or may occur when you are alone. Identify an anxious thought and use this as the basis of your behavioural experiment.

▶ **Step 2: Rate the belief (0–100 per cent)**

Once you have identified the thought you want to test out, rate how strongly you believe that thought on a scale of 0–100 per cent. In the case of anxiety, it may be how much you believe a predicted catastrophic outcome is likely to occur. If you only half-believed it, you would rate that as 50-per-cent belief. If you didn't believe it at all, it would be a rating of 0 per cent, whereas if you really strongly and absolutely believed the thought and that it is definitely what will happen, you would rate this as 100 per cent.

▶ **Step 3: Plan the experiment**

Now that you have identified the exact thought or belief to be tested and you have rated that thought, you need to plan how to test it out. Kayleigh's fear was that, if she met other mums, they would reject her once they got to know her. However, she didn't *know* this as she hadn't yet met them and so had no evidence for this anxiety. Therefore the behavioural experiment for Kayleigh was to go to the coffee morning and see what happened.

Exercise 20

SETTING UP YOUR OWN EXPERIMENT

Think about your own thoughts and situations and write down a behavioural experiment that will allow you to test out the thought and gather evidence for and against it. Write out the experiment below.

1 Identify the 'key' cognition or belief to be tested:

_____

_____

_____

2 Rate the belief (0–100 per cent):

_____

_____

_____

3 Plan the experiment:

_____

_____

_____

_____

_____

 Key points to remember

The behavioural experiment needs to be long enough to provide a fair test. Your experiment needs to have a realistic time frame to provide an accurate test of the thought.

The experiment needs to be doable and realistic. There is no point setting yourself an experiment so challenging that you are unable to complete it. A quick way to test this is to ask yourself how likely you are, on a scale of 1 to 10, to complete this. If the answer is anything less than 7, it is unlikely that you will go ahead. Adjust the timing or the situation enough to make it more comfortable.

Don't make it *too* easy. If you are testing something out and it doesn't feel challenging or difficult in any way, it is unlikely that you are testing something significant or 'key' to your anxiety. That's not to say that behavioural experiments should be unpleasant, but they should challenge a thought that is making you anxious. An experiment that feels really easy is unlikely to reflect a real issue. Go back and review it and ask yourself if you are really focusing on a key problem.

I CAN'T THINK HOW TO TEST MY PROBLEM...

This is a common stumbling block: behavioural experiments are not something we are used to doing in day-to-day life. To give you some ideas, here are a few suggestions.

▶ Ask other people.

A common experiment in CBT is to conduct a survey – either a formal brief questionnaire or informally just asking those around you. For example, if you think you hold an unusual belief or are the only person who worries about something, CBT would say you're not 'allowed' to think that until you have asked other people.

This is a particularly good approach for those 'mind-reading' worries we can hold, such as 'My colleagues will notice my hands shaking during the presentation and think less of me.' In this case CBT would say do the presentation and then find out by asking your colleagues whether they noticed your hands shaking. Again, you are not 'allowed' to have this anxious thought or worry without testing it out first.

▶ **Get some help.**

As well as asking people as part of an experiment, you can ask other people how they think you could test something out and see if those close to you have some good ideas. Remember, though, it has to be significant and meaningful to you and your specific thought, otherwise it will hold little value.

▶ **Ask yourself if you are avoiding.**

Often we *can* think of the exact way to test something, but it feels too scary and so we avoid it. If you think this might be the case for you, go back to the experiment and break down your plan into smaller, more doable steps and see if you are able to work through those instead.

Exercise 21

MONITORING YOUR BEHAVIOURAL EXPERIMENT

This is Step 4 of the experiment, where you use a worksheet to monitor and log your behavioural experiment, either during or immediately after the event. It is important to keep a record of your experiments because it can be hard to remember the details and we want to be able to use this as evidence in the future.

The following worksheet shows the key headings and some instructions to follow in order to complete the right-hand column.

Complete a behavioural experiment, filling in the worksheet (a copy can be found in Appendix 3). Note down any difficulties or problems you encountered and think about how you can overcome these in future experiments. Use Kayleigh's completed example worksheet on the next page as a guide.

Behavioural experiment worksheet	
Date and situation	Write down in detail here when and where you were, who you were with, etc.
Key thought being tested: What do you think will happen?	Write down your key thought/belief that is going to be tested here. Rate how strongly you believe this thought/belief at the time (%).
Experiment: What did you do?	Write down here what you did to test out the thought/ belief.
What did happen?	Write down here what happened during the experiment.
How do you feel now?	Write here how you feel now and anything that you weren't expecting or that surprised you.
Rerated key thought	Re-evaluate that initial key thought/belief and rerate how strongly you believe that thought/belief now (%).

Kayleigh's worksheet	
Date and situation	*3 May: Coffee morning with other mums at local café*
Key thought being tested: What do you think will happen?	*'Once people get to know me they will reject me.' Belief = 100%*
Experiment: What did you do?	*I gave the other mums some information about myself and my husband and our daughter. I told a couple of people that I wasn't working again yet and decided to see what the reaction was. I was as honest as possible because I wanted to test whether people would be interested once they actually got to know more about me.*
What did happen?	*It was a lovely coffee morning. I felt I was honest with everyone and that they got to know the real me. People were really friendly and welcoming and very interested in me and my life/new home, etc.*
How do you feel now?	*Really good! I'm so pleased I went. I felt much more relaxed and chatty than I thought I would after about half an hour and the other mums were very friendly.*
Rerated key thought	*People will not reject me when they get to know me. In fact, people were very interested in me and friendly. I have further invitations to other events which means people must have liked me. I now know my original worry was completely untrue and rate my belief in it as 0%.*

→ # Recording your successes

As well as completing the behavioural experiment worksheets and keeping them as evidence, it is a good idea to complete a brief diary of your successes in completing these experiments. This will boost your confidence and belief in yourself and show you that you are able to try new things and face challenging situations. Next time you have a fear or worry about your ability to do something, you can glance at your record of success and know that you are capable of anything.

Exercise 22

KEEPING A SUCCESS DIARY

As you continue to complete your behavioural experiments, fill in the following record of success diary, using the example given as a guide. Remember to reward your successes.

Date and situation	What I did	How I feel now
3 May: went to coffee morning	Made myself talk to other people and tell them about myself, even though I was worried about this	Confident and happier in myself, and less anxious about the next event

→ Reviewing and repeating experiments

It often takes more than one behavioural experiment to challenge a key cognition. This is because our anxieties are great at putting down our successes and so we need to keep testing out our thoughts and our beliefs until we are satisfied that they were wrong, or until they stop causing us negative emotions. The key is to take the next challenge. Once you have done something successfully, ask yourself if there is another way to test this that may challenge you further or take you one step nearer to your goal.

The most confident people are those who take small risks. By living in our comfort zones all the time, we never find out what we are truly capable of, so go on – push yourself and take the challenge!

WHEN CAN I STOP EXPERIMENTING?

You will be the best judge of whether you can stop testing out a belief. If you feel a sense of avoidance, keep testing until you are able to truly face the challenge you have set yourself.

However, it may be the case that some thoughts need repeated testing at different times and so you may find that throughout life there are times when it is useful to take the challenge and test out a belief or a specific thought. This is fine: you now have the ability and the skills to use this whenever you want, and to overcome any belief or thought that is holding you back. Ideally, you want to keep challenging a thought or belief until it holds an anxiety rating of 0 per cent and no longer causes you distress or anxiety.

What if it goes wrong?

There is no such thing as a behavioural experiment going 'wrong'. Every experience teaches us something valuable and gives us something to reflect on and consider for the future. Don't let fear of failure prevent you from achieving success. Remember: without trying, you've no evidence!

Summary

When conducting a behavioural experiment, we challenge a specific belief in a particular situation, and then carefully monitor the results.

1   Behavioural experiments are important because they provide evidence that is otherwise unattainable.

2   Behavioural experiments can be used not only to disprove negative beliefs and thoughts but also to gain evidence for positive beliefs.

What I have learned

→ What are my thoughts, feelings and insights on what I have read so far?

_____

_____

_____

Use the space below to summarize any actions you identify as a result of reading this chapter.

_____

_____

_____

_____

Where to next?

The next four chapters focus on specific anxiety disorders: panic disorder, phobias, obsessive–compulsive disorder (OCD) and generalized anxiety disorder (GAD). These chapters provide disorder-specific information for these different types of anxiety. Even if you do not have a specific anxiety disorder, it is still useful to read them because they contain many anxiety-busting tips.

7 Working with panic disorder

In this chapter you will learn:
▶ the main symptoms of panic disorder
▶ how to tell whether you have panic disorder by identifying your own panic symptoms
▶ why you have panic attacks, and how to overcome them.

→ What is panic disorder?

Panic disorder is an anxiety disorder where the main symptom is the repeated reoccurrence of panic attacks. Each panic attack will be unexpected, happening seemingly 'out of the blue'. As well as experiencing panic attacks, the sufferer will also be plagued by worry about whether they will have another attack, and if so when and where. This continual worry about having panic attacks and their consequences can make panic disorder very frightening.

When they have a panic attack, people commonly feel intense physical symptoms. As a result, they find it difficult to see how a psychological approach can help. Most people I treat for panic disorder have already been to visit several physicians and undergone investigations for their physical symptoms. For this reason it is important to recognize that a psychological approach is not saying 'it's all in your head'. In the approach described in this chapter there is a strong emphasis on dealing with the physical symptoms of panic, which are in no way dismissed.

When people experience intense panic, those around them may often say 'calm down' or 'just get on with it'. Anyone who has experienced panic will know that dealing with a panic attack is not as straightforward as this. However, you can overcome these attacks, and stop fearing them, through the right use of tools and skills, which this chapter will teach you. These skills will also help reduce the impact of the physical symptoms and ease that physical discomfort as well.

This chapter is based on the work of David Clark's CBT for panic disorder model ('Panic Disorder: from theory to therapy' in *Frontiers of Cognitive Therapy*, P. Salkovskis (ed.) (New York: Guildford Press, 1997). This practical approach to overcoming panic disorder includes behavioural experiments and information about your fears to help you.

Exercise 23

 ## I GET PANICKY, BUT IS IT A PANIC ATTACK?

How do we identify the symptoms of a panic attack versus feeling a bit agitated and panicky?

In order to work out whether or not you are experiencing a panic attack, review the diagnostic criteria below (adapted from the standard US classification, DSM–IV, used by the American Psychiatric Association, 1994) and place a tick next to any symptoms you experience when you panic.

Symptoms of a panic attack	Tick
Palpitations, pounding heart or accelerated heart rate	
Sweating	
Trembling or shaking	
Sensations of shortness of breath or smothering	
Feeling of choking	
Chest pain or discomfort	
Nausea or abdominal distress	
Feeling dizzy, unsteady, light-headed or faint	
Derealization (feelings of unreality) or depersonalization (being detached from oneself)	
Fear of losing control or going crazy	
Fear of dying	
Paresthesias (numbness or tingling sensations)	
Chills or hot flushes	

If you ticked four or more symptoms, it's likely that you have had a panic attack.

The following case study describes one individual's experience of anxiety. Although people may experience many different symptoms during a panic attack, this example illustrates the development and feel of a panic attack.

Sarah's story

'I was in the supermarket and I felt absolutely fine, just doing the usual mid-week dash, and I was on the phone to my husband asking him what we needed and then I suddenly went hot and my heart was racing. I was standing in the middle of the aisle holding the phone but I couldn't talk to my husband. I was trying to tell him that I needed help but I couldn't move my tongue properly, I felt as though I were being choked. I couldn't catch my breath. I stood there clutching my trolley for dear life and all these people were walking by me and I just stood there thinking, "I'm going to die. I'm going to die in the shop. I'm going to collapse in front of all these people and die in the middle of the aisle and people will have to step over me to do their shopping."

'My hands were getting sweaty and I felt really shaky and I just kept thinking, "Oh, no, my hands are too sweaty to hold on, I'm going to collapse and I'll die." I was absolutely certain that if I hit the floor I wouldn't get back up again and would die on the floor and so I was hanging on to my trolley for dear life. A woman shopping with her kids walked by me and she looked at me and said to her kids, "Go and get help," and I just stood there. I couldn't move, I couldn't breathe, I couldn't speak and I just knew I was going to die.

'A manager came with a chair and I sat down and I started to breathe more easily. I just kept thinking, "Thank goodness I'm not on the floor." I felt safe in the chair. Gradually I felt normal again. I told the manager and the other shopper that I felt unwell with a cold and had a temperature, which was a lie, but I didn't know how to explain what had happened. They wanted to call my husband but I just wanted to leave so I said he was meeting me outside and that I was fine. I got into my car and thought, "Wow, I nearly died in there." I haven't told my husband. I don't know how to tell him that I nearly died.'

As you can see from the example above, people experience not only very frightening physical symptoms during a panic attack but also intensely frightening thoughts, such as 'I'm going to die.' Sarah believes her thoughts at this stage and that, if she hadn't been helped into a chair, she wouldn't have survived. She is too frightened to talk to her husband about the fact that she nearly died. We can also recognize some 'safety behaviours' that Sarah has developed, such as not sitting on the floor or lying on it. We'll come back to Sarah later.

The difference between a panic attack and other anxiety is that a panic attack is short-lived. The symptoms listed in the previous exercise will occur in a very intense way, coming on quickly and reaching a peak within ten minutes or so. This makes a panic attack a short but intense period of anxiety.

A surprise attack

'Attack' is a good name for what happens to us when we panic. It is as though the anxiety launches a surprise attack, bringing many different symptoms and a great deal of anxiety all at once. This is why overcoming panic disorder is not as simple as merely 'pulling yourself together'. These are very real symptoms and you will need help and support to overcome them, but the good news is that you *can* overcome them.

> *'Panic at the thought of doing a thing is a challenge to do it.'*
>
> Henry S. Haskins

→ Panic disorder with agoraphobia

Panic disorder can be diagnosed as with or without agoraphobia. Panic disorder with agoraphobia occurs when an individual not only has panic attacks but also experiences anxiety about these panic attacks that prevents them from going out and about, thus interfering with their daily life.

Panic disorder with agoraphobia usually occurs in someone anxious that they will not be able to escape a situation or have ready access to help and support were they to have a panic attack. It is therefore common for those affected to begin to avoid people, places and situations that they think may trigger a panic attack.

Exercise 24

DO I HAVE PANIC DISORDER WITH AGORAPHOBIA?

Listed below are some examples of situations or activities you may be avoiding if you have panic disorder with agoraphobia. Examine the list and tick any that are familiar to you.

Symptoms of panic disorder with agoraphobia	Tick
Being far from home	
Going anywhere without the company of a 'safe' person (e.g. partner or friend)	
Physical activity or exercise (because of the belief that it could trigger a panic attack)	
Going to places where escape is not easy (e.g. restaurants, theatres, stores, public transportation)	
Driving	
Places where it would be embarrassing to have a panic attack, such as a social gathering	
Eating or drinking anything that could possibly provoke panic (such as alcohol, caffeine or certain foods or medications)	

→ What maintains my panic?

As with other anxiety disorders, it is not the symptom of panic itself that maintains the problem but the meaning we attach to it. For example, if we think back to Sarah's eventful visit to the supermarket, we know that she felt the symptoms of a panic attack and interpreted these symptoms as meaning that she was going to die. Sarah also had some thoughts around needing to stay upright because she believed that, if she was on the ground, she would be unable to get back up and would die.

Sarah's interpretations of her symptoms lend some very frightening meanings to them and we can understand why she would be frightened of having another attack. This is the same with any physical symptom we experience. It is easy to misinterpret these experiences and label them as something more frightening or serious than they actually are.

INTERPRETING THE SYMPTOMS

Think back to the symptoms of a panic attack and your own symptoms, and spend some time considering how you interpret those symptoms.

Read carefully through the symptoms listed in the table below. Pay particular attention to the ones that apply to you and write down your own interpretation of these symptoms. An example for the first symptom is included for your guidance.

Symptoms of a panic attack	What does this mean to me?
Palpitations, pounding heart or accelerated heart rate	*There is something wrong with my heart. I will have a heart attack.*
Palpitations, pounding heart or accelerated heart rate	
Sweating	
Trembling or shaking	
Sensations of shortness of breath or smothering	
Feeling of choking	
Chest pain or discomfort	
Nausea or abdominal distress	
Feeling dizzy, unsteady, light-headed or faint	
Derealization (feelings of unreality) or depersonalization (being detached from oneself)	
Fear of losing control or going crazy	
Fear of dying	
Paresthesias (numbness or tingling sensations)	
Chills or hot flushes	

This is not to say the symptoms don't exist: if your heart is pounding, then your heart is pounding; there are no two ways about it. However, if your heart is pounding, this doesn't necessarily mean that anything bad is going to happen, or that there is something wrong with your heart, both of which are common misinterpretations people experience during a panic attack.

→ Why the meaning matters

If we think back to our basic model of CBT explained at the beginning of the book, we know that what we think affects our feelings, our behaviour and our physical symptoms, and that these all interact with one another. When we are dealing with panic disorder, the key component of this interaction is our thoughts. This is because what we think when we experience a panic attack will greatly affect how we feel and behave during an attack. Therefore the focus of treatment is on our thoughts and what we think during the attack.

Focusing on thoughts may seem odd if you are experiencing lots of physical symptoms, but it is important to remember that in CBT all our thoughts, feelings, behaviours and symptoms are linked. Therefore, by changing our thoughts during a panic attack, we *will* be changing our physical symptoms, even if we are not focusing directly on these.

CATASTROPHIC THINKING

Catastrophic thinking, as the name implies, is when something happens and our mind automatically thinks of the worst-case scenario, or a 'catastrophe'. Sometimes we can also have images in our mind of catastrophes, where we imagine or picture the worst happening, and these can form part of our catastrophic thinking. This type of thinking is common in panic disorder and plays a large part in the maintenance of panic attacks.

Catastrophic thinking makes us interpret very minor physical sensations or thoughts as highly significant or dangerous. It makes sense that, if we are interpreting something as dangerous, we will become anxious about it and feel the need to do something about it. This may lead us to develop 'safety behaviour'.

As discussed earlier, safety behaviour is acts or things we use to help us through when we are feeling anxious. When we experience a panic attack, we may use safety behaviour to help us manage the attack or to prevent an attack occurring in the first place. All safety behaviour can reduce the panicky feelings and help us feel safe again, but in the long term it is likely to be maintaining the panic.

Let's take a look at how catastrophic thinking and safety behaviour affect panic attacks.

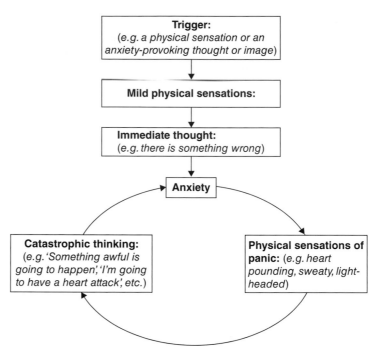

(Diagram adapted from David Clark's model of CBT for panic disorder)

As you can see from the diagram above, the role of catastrophic thinking is significant in creating higher and higher levels of anxiety, which leads to an increase in uncomfortable physical symptoms. Look at the example below, showing how Sarah's catastrophic thinking affected her anxiety.

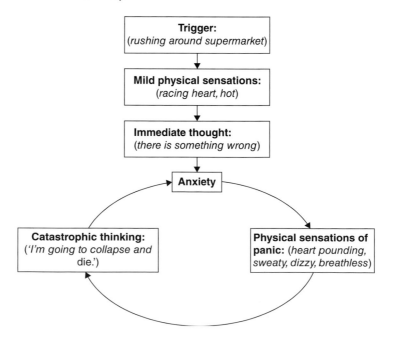

Exercise 26

DRAWING OUT YOUR CATASTROPHIC THINKING

Now consider your own anxiety and panic attacks. Using the examples provided above to guide you, draw out your own catastrophic thinking, using the template below.

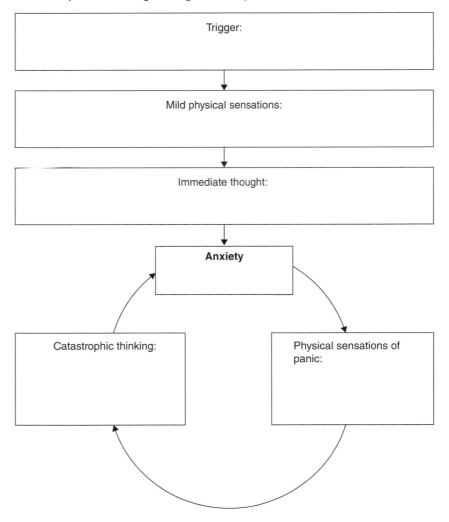

It's possible that several incidents may have led to your panic attacks, so use this template as a guide to draw out the different thoughts or triggers that affect your anxiety and may lead to a panic attack. (A blank copy of this template has been included in Appendix 5 for you to photocopy.)

Exercise 27

BREAKING THE CYCLE OF YOUR PANIC

The first stage is to monitor a panic attack and gather as much information as you can about it.

Remember your last panic attack. Now answer the following questions about that panic attack. Try to be as honest and detailed as possible in your answers – the more information you can provide, the more helpful this exercise will be.

→ My last panic attack:

_____

→ What was the situation? (Where did it happen, when did it happen, who were you with and what actually happened?)

_____

_____

_____

_____

_____

→ What was happening in your body? (What physical sensations did you notice? Were there changes in your body that told you that you were panicking? How did you feel physically?)

_____

_____

_____

_____

➜ What thoughts did you have at the time? (What did you think the physical symptoms meant? What did you think would happen?)

_____

_____

_____

➜ What images did you have at the time? (Did any images of yourself, the situation or anything else come into your mind at the time?)

_____

_____

_____

➜ What was your biggest fear at the time? (What were you worried about happening at the time? Did you worry that you would die or that something bad would happen? What would have been the worst-case scenario?)

_____

_____

_____

➜ How much did you believe your worst-case fear might happen at the time of the panic? Rate this as a percentage, e.g. 'I thought I was going to have a heart attack and at the time I believed this 100 per cent.'

_____

_____

➜ Looking back on it now, how much do you believe your worst-case fear might have happened? Rate your response as a percentage, e.g. 'At the time I thought I was 100 per cent likely to have a heart attack but now I only believe this was 65 per cent likely.'

_____

_____

→ The *real* meaning of physical symptoms

It is important to understand what is happening in your body when you panic. A key part of panic is our misinterpretation of physical symptoms and what they mean. You can do some research on the symptoms of panic to help you better understand your own symptoms, but listed below are the main symptoms, the common misinterpretations and what the symptoms actually mean.

Symptoms of a panic attack	What we think this means	What it actually means
Palpitations, pounding heart or accelerated heart rate	*There is something wrong with my heart.* *I will have a heart attack.*	*Anxiety produces adrenaline as our body gets ready for a 'fight or flight' reaction. This shot of adrenaline increases your heart rate. It shows how strong your heart is and how effectively it is working. Your heart is doing what it is supposed to do.*
Sweating	*I am losing control.*	*Sweating is a normal reaction to the stress hormone cortisol. When we become anxious and stressed, our bodies sweat to alleviate some of this feeling and cool us down.*
Trembling or shaking	*My body is weakening.* *Something is very wrong.*	*When we are anxious, we tense our muscles. This muscle tension causes us to shake but, while we can feel and see this, other people are less likely to notice.* *__Try it:__ Hold your arm straight out in front of you and tense the muscles really tightly and you will notice that your arm starts to shake.*
Feeling of choking	*I can't get enough air.* *I can't swallow.* *I'll die.*	*When we panic, our muscles become tense and this can include muscles in our chest, neck and throat. Alongside this, our short, shallow mouth breathing or hyperventilating makes our mouth feel dry, which can make us feel as though we are choking. Again, our breathing and swallowing reflexes kick in, meaning that we won't choke and nothing bad will happen.*

Symptoms of a panic attack	What we think this means	What it actually means
Sensations of shortness of breath or smothering	*I will choke.* *I will stop breathing.* *I'm dying.*	*When we panic, we don't breathe normally and often take short, sharp breaths, also known as 'hyperventilating'. Because we are not breathing normally, we feel as though we are not getting enough air and this can lead us to panic more and think we will stop breathing. However, breathing is a reflex and, even if we deliberately try to stop breathing, we can't – our body takes over.* ***Try it:** Breathe out slowly and try to resist taking an in-breath for as long as you can. Notice how the reflex kicks in and eventually your body will naturally gasp for air. Even when you try to control your breathing, your body takes over and does the hard work for you.*
Chest pain or discomfort	*I'm having a heart attack.* *Something is wrong with my heart.*	*Although chest pain is frightening, it is caused by muscle tension around your chest, which is caused by the panic and hyperventilating. If you relax your body and your breathing, you'll notice that the pain will go.* ***Try it:** Notice when your chest feels painful or tight and take ten minutes to complete a relaxation or deep-breathing exercise and allow yourself to relax. The pain and discomfort will go.*
Nausea or abdominal distress	*I'm in pain and that means something is wrong.*	*It is perfectly normal to feel sick or have abdominal distress, e.g. an upset stomach, when feeling anxious. This is nothing to worry about and is simply your body's way of trying to get rid of some of the stress hormones and help rebalance you.*

Symptoms of a panic attack	What we think this means	What it actually means
Feeling dizzy, unsteady, light-headed or faint	*I'm going to faint. Something is very wrong with me.*	*The reason we become light-headed or dizzy when we panic is because our breathing changes and we begin to hyperventilate.* ***Try it:*** *Deliberately take short, sharp breaths for three minutes and notice the changes in your body. You will feel light-headed, dizzy and unsteady, but this is normal when you are breathing like this. You won't fall over or lose your balance.*
Derealization (feelings of unreality) or depersonalization (being detached from oneself)	*I'm losing control or going mad.*	*When we experience a shot of adrenaline, as happens when we start to panic, we can experience an odd feeling as though we are removed or detached from our own bodies. This is our body's way of protecting us when it feels threatened and is nothing more than a normal symptom of panic.*
Fear of losing control or going crazy	*I'll do something out of character.* *I have no control over my own body.*	*When we experience symptoms of panic such as trembling, shortness of breath and sweating, we can feel as though our body is going into 'meltdown' and that we are losing control. However, we are not going to suddenly do something out of character because of these feelings. We still have all our normal inhibitions and thoughts in place that stop us 'losing control' and so there is nothing to fear. This is a common fear with panic disorder but it is just a symptom of panic – nothing more.*

Symptoms of a panic attack	What we think this means	What it actually means
Fear of dying	All these symptoms mean I will die.	Often there is a bigger fear underneath the fear of dying, e.g. 'I will leave my children' or 'I will die alone.' Our body is experiencing intense physical symptoms and we think the worst when we panic, which is why this fear comes into our minds. However, thoughts of dying are just that – thoughts. They are no more or less dangerous than planning your weekly shop; they are just thoughts and this doesn't mean you will die.
Paresthesias (numbness or tingling sensations)	Something is wrong in my body. I will lose control of my arms.	This tingling sensation is part of our 'fight or flight' reaction. We experience this because the adrenaline that is delivered to our bodies when we are anxious is preparing our body to fight or flee a situation.
Chills or hot flushes	I'm going to faint. Something bad will happen.	We get hot and cold as a result of the rush of adrenaline and stress hormones, not because anything is physically wrong. Again, this is a common and normal symptom of panic – nothing more.

Having reviewed the different physical symptoms in the table, you can see that, although frightening, they are all due to feelings of panic. We misinterpret these symptoms and think the worst, so we panic more and the symptoms become more acute. This tells you that, although the symptoms can feel very serious, they are in fact the result of acute anxiety, which can be overcome.

The important point here is that this doesn't mean the symptoms are 'all in your head'. The physical symptoms of panic are very real. However, the good news is that, although panic is horrible and frightening, it is not dangerous. Any worries you have about more serious and significant consequences, e.g. having a heart attack, can be dispelled once you know that this is panic. It doesn't make the symptoms any less unpleasant, but it does make them less threatening.

For the next stage, we need to start challenging our thinking around these thoughts and paint a more accurate picture of what is happening to us when we panic. Once we stop focusing on worst-case scenarios and focus instead on the reality, panic attacks are a lot less frightening.

→ Time to consider the evidence

In previous chapters we have talked about the way anxiety will present our thoughts as certain facts. Let's take a moment to remember those principles:

▶ Anxiety causes us to give incorrect meaning to thoughts or images that occur to us.

▶ Anxiety causes us to misinterpret physical symptoms.

▶ Anxiety causes us to have catastrophic thoughts/images and we then believe these to be true.

When we consider the above traits of anxiety and some of the thoughts you listed having during a panic attack, we can begin to see why panic attacks are so nasty. If you are panicking and having the thought 'I'm going to have a heart attack', then you have anxiety telling you that this is true and that you will die – so no wonder you start panicking!

However, we need to acknowledge that these are not facts but anxiety-driven thoughts. We don't have any evidence for these thoughts beyond the physical symptoms, which we are misinterpreting thanks to the anxiety.

CONSIDERING THE 'EVIDENCE'

Take a moment to consider the 'evidence' you have for your feared beliefs. Note it below:

_____

_____

_____

_____

_____

Now consider whether this is real evidence or just anxiety telling you what to think. Review your evidence above and ask yourself whether there is any *actual* evidence that would stand up in a court of law – no guessing or mind reading allowed. Note it below.

_____

_____

_____

If you get stuck, ask a friend or family member to do this with you. Thinking about anxiety can be quite stressful, so it can be helpful to have the support of someone else for this part.

Now consider whether what you experience could be due to panic. It can be difficult to consider strong physical symptoms as 'just' being panic when we are used to thinking of them as being something much more serious, but look back at the table listing common symptoms and misinterpretations. Is it likely that your symptoms could be explained by panic disorder?

→ My symptoms:

_____

_____

_____

_____

→ What they might actually mean:

_____

_____

_____

_____

Start to change your thinking and notice the difference

Once you have identified some of your thinking and physical symptoms as panic disorder, you can use this next time you have, or are worried about having, a panic attack. For example, if you find yourself becoming anxious about panicking, say to yourself:

'This is just panic disorder. Although unpleasant, this is not dangerous and the thoughts and feelings I have are a natural part of panic. If I stay in this situation for 20 to 25 minutes, the panic will start to subside. I can get on with my day, knowing that these are not dangerous symptoms but panic symptoms.'

By having this clarity of thought and being able to reassure yourself in this way, you are preventing the cycle of catastrophic thinking that leads to an increase in symptoms. This means that the panic will be caught early and will begin to subside much more quickly than if we let our train of thought run away to every worst-case scenario we can think of. Remember: you need to challenge your beliefs around the panic and change your thinking.

Exercise 29

KEEPING A PANIC DIARY

Completing a panic diary allows you to monitor your thoughts and symptoms and notice the impact of changing your thoughts at the beginning of a panic attack. What difference does changing your thinking make to your symptoms?

Fill in the monitoring sheet below, or create a separate one of your own. This one includes an example as a guide for your own responses.

Situation	Initial thought	Feeling	Revised thought	Result
Walking the dog, get hot and flustered, heart rate increases	There's something wrong. I'm going to collapse.	Stressed, panicky, anxious	I'm not going to collapse. I am hot from walking the dog and am feeling panicky but this will pass and I will be fine.	Feel much better, symptoms fade, able to carry on as before. Panic very short-lived.

Remember to acknowledge and reward your successes. Facing up to some of your feared beliefs in panic disorder can be a scary business, but you will notice that the more you do this the less frequent panic will become.

→ Get rid of your 'safety' behaviour

In Chapter 5 we discussed how safety behaviour can maintain and worsen anxiety. This is particularly true with panic attacks. Because of our catastrophic thinking, we use safety behaviour to 'manage' our panic and therefore it feels essential.

Let's look again at Sarah's trip to the supermarket. She firmly believed that, if she fell on the floor, she would die, so her safety behaviour was to stay upright or sit on a chair but in no circumstances would she sit on the floor. This led her to believe that the reason she was ok and didn't die was because she hadn't hit the floor, and so this was a maintaining cycle of fear. This is shown in the diagram below:

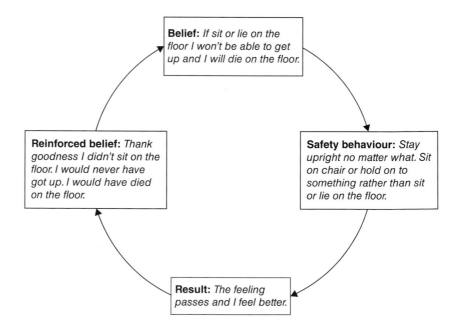

Belief: *If sit or lie on the floor I won't be able to get up and I will die on the floor.*

Safety behaviour: *Stay upright no matter what. Sit on chair or hold on to something rather than sit or lie on the floor.*

Result: *The feeling passes and I feel better.*

Reinforced belief: *Thank goodness I didn't sit on the floor. I would never have got up. I would have died on the floor.*

You can see how Sarah acting in this way was maintaining her belief that the floor is dangerous for her. However, she had no *evidence* for this other than the anxious thoughts. Therefore Sarah needed to ditch her safety behaviour and challenge this belief. She did this by sitting on the floor as soon as she felt her symptoms come on, to see what happened. This was scary for Sarah to do because she believed that, if she were on the floor, she wouldn't get back up again. Initially, she asked her husband to come with her, so that if she got into trouble she knew he could help her.

Sarah then repeated the experiment on her own. Here's what happened:

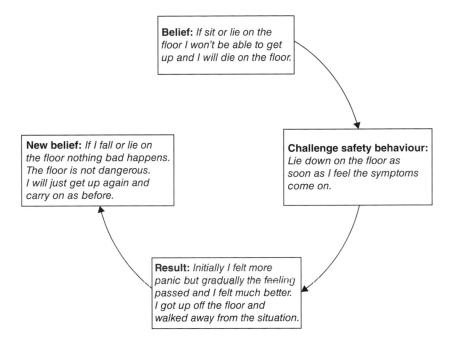

Belief: *If sit or lie on the floor I won't be able to get up and I will die on the floor.*

Challenge safety behaviour: *Lie down on the floor as soon as I feel the symptoms come on.*

Result: *Initially I felt more panic but gradually the feeling passed and I felt much better. I got up off the floor and walked away from the situation.*

New belief: *If I fall or lie on the floor nothing bad happens. The floor is not dangerous. I will just get up again and carry on as before.*

This experience meant that Sarah stopped worrying about falling on the floor because she knew that, if this happened, she would simply get back up again. This small experiment, where Sarah challenged her safety behaviour, showed her that her belief was false and that the safety behaviour was, in fact, maintaining her anxiety about the floor.

→ Take the challenge

Using the principles of behavioural experiments outlined in Chapter 6, plan your own experiments to challenge your safety behaviour. Keep a record of what you thought would happen, what did happen and how you feel about that initial fear now. Remember: you can keep conducting behavioural experiments until you feel you have enough evidence to tell you a situation is safe. By challenging your thinking in this way and ditching your safety behavior, you will discover that situations are safe, that panic passes and that you no longer need to avoid. This is life panic free; enjoy it!

Summary

1 Although deeply unpleasant, panic attacks are not dangerous.

2 Our catastrophic beliefs are what make panic attacks frightening.

3 Review your evidence and ask, 'Have I any proof for this belief?'

4 Challenge your thinking and ditch your safety behaviour.

What I have learned

→ What are my thoughts, feelings and insights on what I have read so far?

_____

_____

_____

Use the space below to summarize any actions you identify as a result of reading this chapter.

_____

_____

_____

_____

Where to next?

This chapter has focused on panic disorder and how to overcome it. The next chapter focuses on specific phobias, how to face your fears and overcome your phobia. If you feel this chapter is not relevant to you, skip ahead to the following chapter.

Working with phobias

In this chapter you will learn:
- ▶ about the nature of phobias and how they develop
- ▶ the difference between a phobia and PTSD
- ▶ some of the key CBT techniques you can employ to help you overcome your phobia.

If you are struggling with a phobia, you will know that it can be hugely distressing. You will go to great lengths to avoid situations where you will be exposed to whatever you fear and will do whatever you need to do to feel safe from your phobia.

Some specific phobias can lead to or be linked with other anxiety disorders. For example, fear of germs can contribute to the development of contamination-based OCD, where a person develops an obsessive fear of germs and subsequent illness. An individual may also develop a fear of public speaking or of humiliating themselves in front of others, and we class this as 'social phobia'.

Phobias can be-far reaching and they may develop for many reasons, and therefore it is important to adapt the principles of this chapter to your own phobia if it is not included here.

'You block your dream when you allow your fear to grow bigger than your faith.'

Mary Manin Morrissey

The principles explained in this chapter follow from Professor Lars-Göran Öst's work on phobia treatment (1989, 1997, Davis, Ollendick & Öst, 2012). Various examples and case studies will be given throughout to help illustrate points.

→ When is a phobia not a phobia?

The difference between a typical response to a stressful situation and an anxiety problem lies in the level of distress experienced by the individual. While it is typical for someone to feel some apprehension or angst about speaking publicly, for example, it is not typical for this situation to cause undue worry or anxiety and subsequent distress. When these stronger emotional reactions are experienced, it is likely that this situation has developed into a phobia. A fear becomes a phobia when the level of distress and the avoidance of the object or situation interfere with our day-to-day life.

Occasionally a person may develop a phobia after a traumatic event, e.g. a fear of flying may occur as a result of a stressful flight. It is important to recognize the difference between a phobia and post-traumatic stress disorder (PTSD). PTSD also occurs after a traumatic event and can lead to a person feeling very anxious and distressed, and this distress may be 'triggered' by specific stimuli, people or places. As such, this can be mistaken for a phobia, but the treatment for PTSD is quite different and so it is important to understand whether what you are experiencing is PTSD or a specific phobia.

Look at the criteria for PTSD below and see whether these are familiar feelings, symptoms or experiences for you. If they are, you may need to seek additional help from your GP, although the anxiety-management techniques explained elsewhere in this book will still be of use to you and allow you to better manage your anxiety while you seek treatment for your PTSD.

PHOBIA OR PTSD?

If you have been exposed to a traumatic event, you may have PTSD rather than a phobia. Review the symptoms below and tick the ones that you think apply to you.

Exposure to the event	Reaction/symptoms	Tick
You have experienced, witnessed or been confronted with an event or events that involve actual or threatened death or serious injury, or a threat to the physical integrity of yourself or others.	Intense fear, helplessness or horror	
Remembering the event	Reaction/symptoms	
You persistently re-experience the traumatic event in at least one of the following ways:	• Recurrent and intrusive distressing recollections of the event, including images, thoughts or perceptions • Recurrent distressing dreams of the event • Acting or feeling as if the traumatic event were recurring; also known as flashbacks (these include a sense of reliving the experience and having illusions, hallucinations) • Intense psychological distress at exposure to internal or external cues that symbolize or resemble an aspect of the traumatic event, i.e. something that reminds you of the event • Strong physical reaction upon exposure to internal or external cues that symbolize or resemble an aspect of the traumatic event	

Avoiding reminders of the event	Reaction/symptoms	
You try to avoid anything associated with the trauma	• *Efforts to avoid thoughts, feelings, conversations, activities, places or people that remind you of the trauma* • *Blanking out details of the event or an important aspect of it* • *Noticeable loss of interest or participation in activities that were important to you or that you previously enjoyed* • *Feeling of detachment, disconnection or estrangement from others* • *Feeling numb* • *Unable to think about the future (e.g. not expecting to have a career, marriage, children or a normal lifespan)*	
Hyper-arousal	Reaction/symptoms	
You have persistent symptoms of increasing arousal (not present before the trauma), indicated by at least two of the following:	• *Difficulty falling or staying asleep* • *Irritability or outbursts of anger* • *Difficulty concentrating* • *Hyper-vigilance* • *Exaggerated startle response, e.g. people or noises make you jump and feel more tense or on edge*	

(Adapted from DSM-IV)

If you recognize some or all of the symptoms above, and you can recall a significant event that may have triggered these feelings, it is possible that you are suffering from PTSD. PTSD is a treatable condition but it requires specialist therapy. You should make an appointment with your doctor to discuss this and request a referral for specific therapy for PTSD.

If you do not recognize the symptoms above but do recognize that you have a phobia, continue to work your way through this chapter to help you face your fear and overcome your phobia.

→ How did my phobia start?

Phobias can start for many different reasons. We often begin to develop them as children, when we first become aware of those around us and how they react to different objects or situations. Phobias can typically begin in children as young as four years old and then continue to develop as we get older.

Phobias often arise because we see people around us become fearful of an object or situation and so we begin to think of that object or situation as something to be afraid of or feared. For example, if we see other people react fearfully to spiders, we may become frightened of them ourselves. Unless we have an experience to disqualify that fear, we can become increasingly fearful as we get older.

 Top tip: if you notice a phobia developing in a child, it's good to get them used to whatever they are scared of before they get older and develop a full-blown phobia.

Why am I afraid of some things and not others?

This will depend on how your phobia developed and what you learned about specific objects or situations that made you fearful of them. For example, although I had a fear of spiders I was absolutely fine with any other bugs or insects. When my friend Ben left his car with the windows open under a tree with a wasps' nest in it while we were camping, I was the one who got into the car full of wasps and drove around until they left the car and it was 'safe' for Ben to get back into the vehicle. As he did so, he said to me, 'Steph, you are so brave!' I remember telling him, 'I'm not brave, I'm just not scared of wasps. If that'd been a car full of spiders, I'd have run a mile!'

Phobias are not an overall 'weakness' or inability to cope. They are specific to specific objects or situations. It is important to remember that, just because a situation or object frightens you, you are still a brave person in other ways and cope with things that other people do not. It is important to remember this because phobias can make us feel foolish and dent our confidence.

HOW BRAVE AM I?

Take a few moments now to think of some examples where you have been brave or done something that other people wouldn't have. Write them in the table below.

Situation	How I dealt with it

Now that you have identified situations in your life that you are able to deal with without fear, stop comparing yourself unfavourably with other people. Specific phobias are just that: specific. They are specific to you and to a circumstance or object. Therefore your friend may well be fine with spiders but may have fears that are less obvious, such as fear of public speaking.

→ You are not alone with your phobia

When we are afraid of things that those around us don't seem bothered by, we can feel very foolish and isolated. However, research shows that around 8 per cent of the UK and US adult population are affected by phobias (and those are just the ones who admit it – the real figure is likely to be higher!). Therefore, many people are afraid of something to a degree where it causes them huge distress and interferes with their day-to-day life. That is not to say the other 92 per cent are living without fears: it is rather that the fears have not reached 'phobia' level, i.e. they are not severe enough to meet diagnostic criteria. However, they may still be distressing for that individual.

The ten most commonly reported phobias in the UK, according to a survey by the charity Anxiety UK, are:

- social phobia: fear of interacting with other people
- agoraphobia: fear of open public spaces
- emetophobia: fear of vomiting
- erythrophobia: fear of blushing
- driving phobia: fear of driving
- hypochondria: fear of illness
- aerophobia: fear of flying
- arachnophobia: fear of spiders
- zoophobia: fear of animals
- claustrophobia: fear of confined spaces.

In the US the picture is similar, with fear of heights (acrophobia) and fear of thunderstorms (brontophobia) also being commonly reported.

You may spot your phobia listed here, in which case know that you are not alone: you have one of the most common phobias. When reading down the list, you may also have thought, 'How can anyone be scared of that?!' This is a common reaction to phobias and explains why other people do not always understand or support our phobias: they simply don't *get* why someone is afraid of that object or situation. This is ok. They don't need to understand *why* you are afraid; they just need to be able to support you through it.

Throughout this chapter you will find tips on how others can support you through your therapy for phobias.

→ Why can't I just get over it?

A phobia goes beyond a dislike of the object or situation. A phobia means that even the thought of coming into contact with or having to face what we are afraid of can cause extreme and irrational fear and dread, leading us to feel completely panic-stricken. Often the phobia and the fear will take priority over anything else. An example might be someone on their wedding day who won't walk up the aisle because she spots a spider in the corner of the church and needs it to be removed before she will get married.

Do not make the mistake of thinking this is just weakness or that you can just 'get over' this by yourself. A phobia causes such feelings of panic and anxiety that it is extremely difficult to manage without specific help or strategies. It is important to recognize this and to realize just how brave you are being even to *think* about overcoming your phobia.

I DON'T HAVE TO TOUCH IT, DO I?

This is a question I am often asked by people who are afraid of an animal or object. One common misconception about therapy for phobias is that it will use a technique called 'flooding'. Flooding involves completely immersing the phobic in the dreaded situation or feared object until they no longer feel panicky and are over their phobia.

This is based on the principle, explained earlier, that anxiety can be maintained for only a certain period of time. Had someone stuck me in a room full of tarantulas and not let me out for 24 hours when I had a fear of spiders, eventually my anxiety around spiders would have faded; but I wouldn't have thanked them for it!

This is the problem with flooding. Although it can be a very effective technique, it is not popular with patients (understandably) and the thought of such a situation can be enough to put people off even coming for therapy, or tackling their phobia to begin with. This is why a different approach is taken in CBT for phobias – an approach called 'graded exposure'.

Graded exposure is a gentler approach, where we work towards facing our feared object or situation in a controlled and manageable way, getting rid of our fear and anxiety bit by bit. No flooding is involved. The answer to the question is therefore yes, you may have to touch the animal or go into the situation you fear, but you will feel good doing it and will only do this when you are ready and prepared.

 *Exercise 32*

 ## CHALLENGING OUR PHOBIC THINKING

When we are scared, our anxiety presents information to us as truth, despite the fact that we have no actual *evidence* to back it up. Therefore the exposure during therapy is used to challenge some of the ideas that our anxiety has given us as facts. It allows us to test out our anxious beliefs.

Use the table below to identify your phobia and some of the 'facts' that anxiety presents you with. I have given examples from my own experience to get you started.

Phobia	'Facts' that anxiety told me were true
Fear of spiders	If I touch a spider, it will run up my arm towards my face. Spiders will run across a room towards me. Spiders will get trapped in my hair.

Now ask yourself, honestly, whether you have any direct evidence of any of these 'facts' happening to you. Things you have read online or that a friend of a friend told you do not count. This is about concrete evidence and direct experience that you have about these facts.

→ How to tackle your phobia

Whenever I work with phobias, it never ceases to amaze me just how much information and how many 'facts' a person can gather on one topic. However, what amazes me even more than the amount of information is the really fantastical beliefs that people hold about their feared object or situation.

I was the same with spiders. I had half-remembered stories people had told me and 'facts' that I had seen on TV, all of which had fuelled some really unhelpful beliefs about spiders and what they are capable of. When faced with a spider, I also tended to give it very negative personality traits such as being vindictive or 'out to get me'. The poor spider was just minding its own business and I had it painted as the villain of the century!

Beware bogus sources of information

This was brought home to me when I mentioned to some colleagues that I am not keen on flying. It was an off-the-cuff comment and I was referring to the fact that I don't like the pressure change that makes my ears 'pop' when flying, rather than fear of flying itself. Before I'd finished my sentence, everyone was telling me their horror stories: plane crashes they'd read about or a friend of a friend who had experienced or witnessed something awful to do with a plane and how upsetting it was. I remember thinking to myself, 'It's a good thing I'm ok with flying.'

People are very ready to tell you all kinds of horrible things that will validate your fears, but beware of unreliable sources of information. Unless they are experts in the field, they are not going to know and could be repeating false information. Any actual facts will be completely misplaced.

Exercise 33

STOP BELIEVING AND START DISCOVERING

It's time to sit down and gather some facts about your feared object/situation. The phrase 'know your enemy' applies here: the more you know about your feared object or situation, the less anxious and vulnerable you will feel.

The following diagram shows some of the facts I discovered about spiders through therapy.

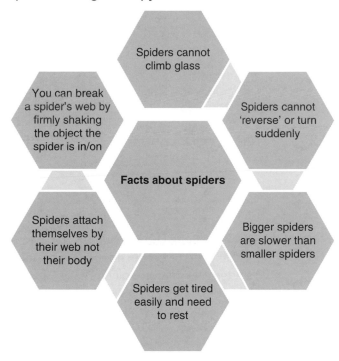

Start investigating, using reliable sources of knowledge, and find out some facts about your own feared object or situation.

Complete the following diagram, highlighting the facts that you have uncovered about your feared object or situation.

Get help with your fact-finding. You may be worried about looking into the topic or situation due to a fear of coming across scary images, e.g. pictures or videos of spiders on YouTube. Ask someone you trust to help you research this topic, or contact Anxiety UK or the Anxiety and Depression Association of America (see contacts list at the end of the book) who may be able to provide you with helpful information about your phobia.

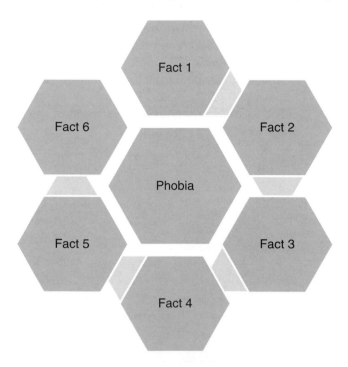

Consider the facts you have uncovered. Do any of them challenge your initial fears or beliefs about your phobia? I personally discovered that spiders act in a very different way from the way I thought they did. However, I had some beliefs that spiders might act differently around *me,* and so I needed to get up close and personal to discover more about them.

→ Fill gaps in your knowledge

Although you may have disproved some of your own beliefs through fact-finding, there will probably be many gaps in your knowledge. For example, while I was convinced that, if I stayed in a room with a spider in it, it would run towards me and crawl up me, I had never stayed in a room with a spider in it long enough to find out! These gaps in my knowledge showed me that, although I had a very real fear of spiders, I didn't know much about the actual 'threat' they posed. I was afraid of spiders without knowing whether I actually needed to be.

Unless something has directly happened to you, you cannot *know* that this happens. You will have gaps in your knowledge. Unless you have information from relevant and reliable sources, a lot of what you 'know' about your feared object or situation may in fact be nonsense.

Exercise 34

HIGHLIGHTING THE GAPS IN YOUR KNOWLEDGE

Look again at some of the beliefs and 'facts' you identified about your feared object and recognize some of the gaps in your knowledge about your phobia.

Use the table below to highlight the gaps in your knowledge and the questions you are left with. Use the example given as a guide.

Phobia	Belief about phobia	Gap in knowledge	Question I am left with
Spiders	Spiders will run across a room and crawl up me.	Yes – never stayed to find out	If I stay in a room with a spider, will it run across the room and crawl up me?

→ Using graded exposure

No matter how tempting, you cannot skip this part. Remember: the key word here is *graded* exposure. The idea of graded exposure is that you work with the fear until you overcome it in a manageable and controlled way. By deliberately exposing yourself gradually to this situation, you will be able to overcome your fear in a safe environment. This means that, if you came across your feared object or situation unexpectedly, you will no longer have the fear and so will be able to cope with it.

Before you begin, you need to undertake to do the following:

1 Commit

You need to commit yourself to staying in the situation, no matter how anxious you feel, until you have completed each part of your graded exposure.

2 Rate your anxiety

It is important to rate your anxiety so that you can monitor progress as you go.

3 Be brave

Remember, it is anxiety that is telling you that you cannot do this and that it is dangerous; these are just anxious beliefs, not facts.

4 Reward yourself

This is important! You will have just done something really brave and you need to recognize this and reward yourself accordingly. Write out a list of rewards that you are going to treat yourself to at every stage – this will give you an additional boost when things get challenging.

Exercise 35

PREPARING A HIERARCHY

Your exposure hierarchy provides the basis for graded exposure. The hierarchy starts with the least anxiety-provoking situation and moves upwards to the most anxiety-provoking situation. You can have as many steps on your hierarchy as you wish, but you need to ensure that each one presents some level of challenge. Without the challenge you are not proving anything to yourself and therefore not making progress.

Here is an example of a graded exposure hierarchy.

Most anxiety-provoking

Having a spider in my hair

Having a spider on my face

Holding a spider in my hands

Trapping a spider under a glass and putting it outside

Being next to a live spider that is trapped under a glass

Being within a metre (3 ft) of a live spider

Holding a dead spider

Least anxiety-provoking

Looking at pictures/ watching videos of spiders

Now complete your own hierarchy in the space below, including as many steps as you need, ranging from least anxiety-provoking to most anxiety-provoking.

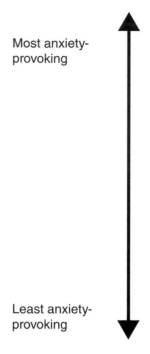

Most anxiety-
provoking

Least anxiety-
provoking

 If you struggle to think of steps in between, ask someone else for their input. Sometimes when we are dealing with our own phobia, it can be hard to think of the stages in between because everything feels challenging and anxiety-provoking, so someone else's perspective is helpful.

→ **Taking the plunge**

Now you start to expose yourself to your feared situation or object. Remember the four key points. Accept that this is going to be uncomfortable but that you are committed to staying in the situation until you complete all the stages.

As different anxious thoughts arise, use the opportunity to perform a behavioural experiment (see Chapter 6) to help you challenge these anxious beliefs. To begin with, it can be a good idea to have someone with you, perhaps a friend, partner or colleague. This is particularly important if you are fearful of a particular object or creature because that person can help collect the object, e.g. a spider, and keep it for you.

Exercise 36

WORKING THROUGH YOUR HIERARCHY

Look at the least anxiety-provoking step in your hierarchy and set some time aside to begin with this task. *Don't delay:* the longer you put this off, the longer your anxiety has to get into your head, which will make this harder for you.

Complete this first step of your hierarchy using the following worksheet. As you begin each stage, you need to rate your anxiety out of 100 and you need to repeat the task until you can do it with a rating of 0/100. The idea of this is that, once you are completely comfortable with one stage, you will be ready to move on to the next.

Use the worksheet below to monitor your progress and keep track of your anxiety ratings as you work your way through your hierarchy. Use the example given as a guide.

Graded exposure worksheet				
Exposure task	Anxiety rating /100	When task was completed	Anxiety rating with each repetition	How I feel now
Hold a dead spider	60	My partner found a dead spider and he held it first, then put it on my hand briefly then took it off. Kept repeating this until I felt better and could hold the spider without any fear.	60/100 50/100 50/100 20/100 0/100	Nothing bad happened. I feel really brave!

By working your way through your hierarchy, you will find yourself able to deal with situations that previously would have filled you with dread. You will also find that, contrary to what you may think, each stage becomes easier rather than harder. This is because you have already completed tasks that previously felt impossible and this fills you with confidence and courage for the next stage.

Warning: Don't stop!

It's tempting to get so far up the hierarchy and think to yourself, 'Well, that's good enough; I'll stop there,' without completing the hierarchy. However, this isn't enough because there will still be some fear remaining. In my case I never thought I would sit there coolly with a spider in my hair but I felt very comfortable and was more concerned for the spider than for myself. (Top tip: tilt your head forward and gently shake your head and the spider will calmly drop down in front of you.)

Having completed my hierarchy, I felt on top of the world and this has given me the confidence to know that I have nothing to fear. Now, were I to come across a spider, I could calmly put it outside with no anxiety.

→ Continue to challenge yourself

Once you have completed your hierarchy and have faced your feared object or situation, it is important to continue to expose yourself to it. The more you do this, the more comfortable and confident you will be and soon the phobia will cease to exist. I have continued to deal with spiders myself, even when someone else has offered to put them outside for me. I knew I was truly over my fear of spiders when I started to put them outside for other people who were afraid, without even thinking about it. Result!

Remember to reward yourself

It takes courage to complete this process, but experiencing a few moments of fear that help you overcome your phobia are much better than living with lifelong fear. The hierarchy principle is a way of approaching any frightening situation by breaking it down into steps, completing each step until you are anxiety-free and then moving on to the next stage.

Summary

1 Anxiety will give you plenty of 'facts' about your feared object or situation but, unless you have direct personal experience, you have no evidence to support these.

2 You can tackle your phobia bit by bit, overcoming it in stages. Completing each stage helps give you the confidence you need to tackle the next one in your hierarchy.

3 This principle can be applied to many different feared situations; break it down and challenge each one, one step at a time.

What I have learned

→ What are my thoughts, feelings and insights on what I have read so far?

_____

_____

_____

Use the space below to summarize any actions you identify as a result of reading this chapter.

_____

_____

_____

_____

Where to next?

The next chapter focuses on obsessive–compulsive disorder (OCD) and how to overcome it. If you feel this chapter is not relevant to you, then skip ahead to Chapter 10.

Working with obsessive–compulsive disorder (OCD)

There are a great many inaccurate portrayals of OCD in the media and these have led to thousands of people thinking they have OCD when they don't. OCD seems to have become a 'fashionable' disorder, with many people saying 'Oh, I'm a bit like that', when there is nothing wrong with their mental health.

For example, many people will describe themselves as 'a bit OCD' if they like things done in a certain order or if they like to keep their homes clean and tidy. This is not OCD. It is perfectly normal to have preferences for order and routine, and cleanliness works on a sliding scale, with some people being very particular and other people being a lot more relaxed about their cleaning. Despite what the media will tell you, it is perfectly possible to have an immaculate home, have all your CDs alphabetized and have all your books lined up in height order and *not* have OCD.

The difference between liking your surroundings to be neat and tidy and having OCD (which, by the way, is not all about neatness, tidiness and cleanliness – but more on that later) is the level of distress felt by the individual. Those suffering from OCD will develop rituals or 'compulsions' which they need to carry out and will become extremely distressed if they are unable to do so. Whereas many people who like things neat and tidy may experience some discomfort if things are messy, they won't feel *distressed* by the situation. However, someone with OCD cannot tolerate the level of distress that accompanies the situation and would have to act to resolve it. My patients with OCD will describe a *need* to complete their rituals, saying 'Even if someone put a gun to my head and told me to stop, I couldn't.'

 It is not possible to address all aspects of OCD in a single chapter, but we need to understand that OCD goes way beyond cleaning and has huge and devastating impacts on individuals' lives, which is why the media message of 'I'm a bit like that' is so unhelpful and misleading. There's no such thing as a 'bit' OCD.

This chapter is based on the work of Rachman & de Silva (2009), Rachman (2003), Salkovskis (1997) and Purdon & Clarke (2005).

> *'A man who fears suffering is already suffering from what he fears.'*
>
> Michel de Montaigne

→ So what *is* OCD?

As the name suggests, obsessive–compulsive disorder has two main components: 'obsessions' and 'compulsions'.

WHAT ARE OBSESSIONS?

Obsessions are recurrent and persistent thoughts, impulses or images that are intrusive, inappropriate and cause anxiety or distress. They pop into your mind and are not easily dismissed so that, even if you manage to distract yourself from the thoughts for a short while, they will return.

The thoughts, impulses or images are not simply excessive worries about real-life problems. For example, these won't be everyday worries about finances or illness, which may be related to real-life events. Instead, these will be worries about things that may never happen or things that other people would never think to worry about.

The person having these obsessions will often attempt to ignore or suppress such thoughts, impulses or images, or to neutralize them with some other thought or action (a compulsion). The person recognizes that the obsessional thoughts, impulses or images are a product of his or her own mind (not imposed from someone or something else).

This is the big difference between OCD and psychosis. Individuals with OCD and psychosis may both report urges or images or sometimes voices that tell them something is wrong or to do something. However, the person with OCD will on some level have insight into their problem and situation. Often people will say to me 'I know this is crazy but I can't seem to stop doing it,' or ' I *know* nothing bad will happen, I *know* this is just in my head ... but I do these things just in case.' This is classic OCD thinking and the 'just in case' element is something which we will come to later on. Those with psychosis lack this insight into their own mental health and the impact of their thoughts and compulsions.

WHAT ARE COMPULSIONS?

Compulsions are repetitive behaviours, such as hand washing, ordering and checking, or mental acts, such as praying, counting or repeating words silently, that the person feels driven to perform in response to an obsession (intrusive thought) or according to rules that must be applied rigidly. People who carry out these compulsions or behaviours will often have a set way of doing things. There will be a 'correct' way to wash or dress or drive to work and so on. If the compulsive action is disturbed or interrupted, the person may feel they need to start it again. This often means that people carry out their compulsions in secret, or develop ways of ensuring they can carry them out without other people knowing or without being interrupted.

Sometimes the behaviour or mental acts are aimed at reducing distress or preventing some dreaded event or situation. However, these behaviours or mental acts may not be connected in a realistic way with what they are designed to neutralize or prevent, or they could be clearly excessive. For example, a mother may worry about accidentally poisoning her children and therefore may wash her hands repeatedly throughout the day whenever she touches anything, even if it is clean. So she may even wash her hands in between unloading clean items from the dishwasher.

Since compulsions can be not only physical acts that people carry out, but thoughts, words or prayers that people say inside their heads, it may not always be obvious when someone is carrying out a compulsion.

Exercise 37

DO I HAVE OCD?

You may be wondering whether you even have OCD. The following questionnaire is often used to help people identify OCD symptoms (Foa *et al.*, 2002). The purpose of this questionnaire isn't to provide you with a 'score' – there isn't necessarily a number that will determine whether you have OCD or not – but completing the questionnaire will highlight any OCD symptoms you have and indicate to what extent they affect you.

Symptom	Do you have this thought?	How much does this thought distress you? (0 = not at all, 1 = a little, 2 = moderately, 3 = a lot, 4 = extremely)
Unpleasant thoughts come into my mind against my will and I cannot get rid of them.		
I think contact with bodily secretions (perspiration, saliva, blood, urine, etc.) may contaminate my clothing or somehow harm me.		
I ask people to repeat things to me several times, even though I understood the first time.		
I wash and clean obsessively.		
I mentally go over past events, conversations and actions to make sure that I didn't do or say something wrong.		
I have saved up so many things that they get in the way.		
I check things more often than necessary.		
I avoid using public toilets because I am afraid of disease or contamination.		

Symptom	Do you have this thought?	How much does this thought distress you? (0 = not at all, 1 = a little, 2 = moderately, 3 = a lot, 4 = extremely)
I repeatedly check doors, windows, drawers, etc.		
I repeatedly check gas and water taps and light switches after turning them off.		
I collect things I don't need.		
I have thoughts of having hurt someone without knowing it.		
I have thoughts that I might want to harm myself or others		
I get upset if objects are not arranged properly.		
I feel obliged to follow a certain order when undressing, dressing or washing myself.		
I feel compelled to count while I am doing things.		
I am afraid of impulsively doing embarrassing or harmful things.		
I need to pray to cancel bad thoughts or feelings.		
I keep on checking forms or other things I have written.		
I get upset at the sight of scissors, knives and other sharp objects in case I lose control with them.		
I am excessively concerned about cleanliness.		
I find it difficult to touch an object when I know it has been touched by strangers or by certain people.		
I need things to be arranged in a particular order.		

→ Different types of OCD

Listed below are some of the different types of OCD. You may feel you can relate to one or more of these categories, or 'subtypes', of OCD.

CONTAMINATION

Those affected by this type of OCD will experience feelings of discomfort associated with contamination and may wash or clean excessively to reduce their feelings of distress. For example, you might feel that your hands are dirty or contaminated after touching a door handle or worry that you will contaminate others with your germs. To get rid of these feelings, you might wash your hands repeatedly.

Within this category sits the 'mental contamination' category. Mental contamination refers to a similar feeling of dirt or contamination but without the physical contact. In other words, sometimes we can be made to *feel* dirty even though we haven't touched something. This may be due to thinking or seeing something distasteful, seeing someone we dislike, or thinking something inappropriate. When experiencing mental contamination, we may attempt to deal with it in the same way as physical contamination by excessively washing or showering until we feel clean again.

RUMINATIONS

People experiencing rumination often have intense thoughts related to possible harm to themselves or others and use checking rituals to relieve their distress. For example, we might imagine our house burning down and then continually drive by our house to make sure that there is no fire. In addition, we may feel that, by simply thinking about a disastrous event, we are increasing the likelihood of such an event happening.

'PURE O'

These are obsessions without visible compulsions, or so-called 'pure obsessions'.

This symptom subtype often relates to unwanted obsessions surrounding sexual, religious or aggressive themes. For example, we could experience intrusive thoughts about being a rapist or a paedophile or that we will attack someone. This is called 'Pure O', as people often describe themselves as not carrying out compulsions when they have these thoughts.

However, we may often use mental rituals such as reciting particular words, counting or praying to relieve the anxiety we experience when we have these involuntary thoughts. Triggers related to obsessions are usually avoided at all costs.

'JUST RIGHT'

These are obsessions with ordering, symmetry, arranging and counting.

We may feel a strong need to arrange and rearrange objects until they are 'just right'. For example, we might feel the need to constantly arrange our shirts so that they are ordered precisely by colour. This symptom subtype can also involve thinking or saying sentences or words over and over again until a task is accomplished perfectly. There is often no quantifiable number as to how many times these rituals should be completed; instead, we carry them out until things feel 'just right'.

HOARDING

Hoarding used to be considered part of OCD and by some professionals is still included in this category, although a new classification shows hoarding as related to but separate from OCD. Hoarding involves the collection of items that are judged to be of limited value by others, such as old magazines, clothes, receipts, junk mail, notes or containers.

With hoarding, it is common for living space to become so cluttered that it becomes impossible to live in. Hoarding is often accompanied by obsessional fear of losing items or possessions that may be needed one day and excessive emotional attachment to objects. Hoarders are likely to experience high anxiety and depression and often encounter huge interference with day-to-day living. NB: Compulsive hoarding can occur independently of OCD.

→ When and why did I develop OCD?

It is common for people to develop OCD or OCD symptoms around a time of increased responsibility. For example, starting secondary school, leaving home, going to university, starting a new job, becoming a parent: these are all times when we perceive ourselves as more responsible and may therefore be vulnerable to developing OCD.

This does not mean that you *will* develop OCD at these points; obviously many people go through these life events without developing OCD. However, there is a vulnerability to developing OCD that occurs at this time as a result of our perceived sense of increased obligation or commitment.

WHAT MAINTAINS MY OCD?

It is important to recognize that you are not alone in having distressing thoughts. Research has repeatedly shown that individuals both with and without OCD will experience the same thoughts. For example, it is common for everyone to experience fleeting thoughts of a violent, sexual or blasphemous nature. However, the difference when someone with OCD has these thoughts is that *they apply a meaning to the thought*. They believe that the thought says something about them.

	Person without OCD	Person with OCD
Thought	*'I might run those children over.'*	
Appraisal	*No appraisal of thought or meaning given*	*'Oh my goodness, I've had that thought because I secretly want to run those children over. I am a dangerous person.'*
Behaviour	*Thought is easily dismissed and behaviour doesn't change*	*Thought causes distress, is not easily dismissed, behaviour changes and person changes their route to work so they do not drive past the school – just in case.*

As you can see from the example above, the thought itself is not unique to OCD. Everyone has fleeting thoughts of a disturbing or distressing nature. The difference is that someone with OCD will interpret having those thoughts as meaning something about them.

 *Exercise 38*

IDENTIFYING THE MEANING OF YOUR THOUGHTS

It is important to identify the meaning you apply to the thoughts or images you are having. A key part of the therapy for OCD is not challenging the *content* of the thoughts, but rather the *meaning* you apply to them.

Use the table below to write down some of the thoughts or images you have had and the meaning you have attached to them. An example has been given to help you.

Situation	Thought/image	The meaning I give that thought/image
Holding baby and looking out of the window	*Image of opening window and throwing baby out of the window*	*'I am a danger to this baby and shouldn't hold him in case I throw him out of the window.'*

Attaching meaning to thoughts creates a cycle that maintains the anxiety and the OCD. The meaning we attach to a thought directly affects our emotional response to it and our subsequent behaviour.

THE THOUGHTS–APPRAISAL–BEHAVIOUR CYCLE

Consider the CBT formulation diagram at the beginning of this book that looked at the impact our thoughts have on our behaviour, physical symptoms and feelings. The example shown below demonstrates that cycle using the example given above.

Situation: Holding baby near window

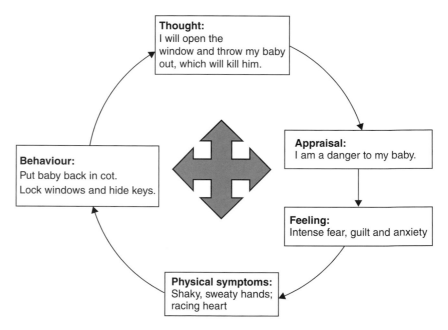

Thought: I will open the window and throw my baby out, which will kill him.

Appraisal: I am a danger to my baby.

Feeling: Intense fear, guilt and anxiety

Physical symptoms: Shaky, sweaty hands; racing heart

Behaviour: Put baby back in cot. Lock windows and hide keys.

By identifying the meaning that is keeping your OCD active, you can begin to challenge the OCD. The first stage of this is to get a realistic 'snapshot' of your OCD and the impact it is having on you, by monitoring and recording your thoughts and behaviour.

Now consider your own appraisals and the impact that these may be having and add your notes to the cycle below.

Situation: _____

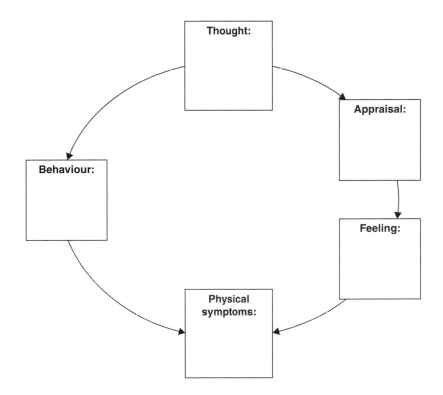

RECORDING OUR THOUGHTS AND BEHAVIOUR

To gain the information we need to begin to challenge the OCD, we need to record our thoughts and behaviour over a week. This only works if we are completely honest with ourselves about what the OCD is driving us to do so, when completing the record, try to be as honest as possible.

Record your thoughts, feelings and behaviour, either in the table below or on a tablet or smartphone. You will get a much more accurate and detailed picture if you record things as they happen.

You may discover that you are engaged in a lot more OCD thinking or behaving than you thought. Do not be put off by this – it's very common and doesn't make your OCD any less treatable.

An example has been given to help get you started, and a blank version of the table is available in Appendix 3.

Situation	Thought	Feeling	Behaviour	Result
Babysitting my niece and about to bath her	'I might drop her in the bath and she will hit her head and drown.'	Panic Anxiety	Don't bath her and instead wait for my brother to do it	Feel bad for letting my brother down and sad to miss out but relieved that I didn't hurt my niece

→ Thinking errors in OCD

Listed below are some common thinking errors that apply specifically to those affected by OCD. Review the list and consider which of these errors apply to you and your thinking.

Intolerance of uncertainty: You feel as if you *must* have a 100-per-cent guarantee of safety or absolute certainty. Any hint of doubt or ambiguity, or the possibility of negative outcome (however small) is unacceptable. This is the core distortion of OCD.

Overestimation of threat: You exaggerate the probability that a negative outcome will occur; or you exaggerate the seriousness of any negative consequences.

Overestimation of responsibility: You believe that, because you think about harmful consequences, you are therefore responsible for preventing harm from coming to yourself or others. Failure to prevent (or failure to try to prevent) harm is the same thing as causing harm.

Significance of thoughts: You believe that your negative obsessional thoughts are overly important or very meaningful. For example, you may think that there is something seriously wrong with your brain because you have senseless thoughts.

Moral thought–action fusion: You believe that your unwanted thoughts are morally equivalent to performing a terrible action. You think you are an awful, immoral or disgraceful person for thinking these thoughts.

Likelihood thought–action fusion: You believe that thinking certain thoughts increases the chance that something terrible will happen. For example, 'If I think about death, someone will die.'

Need to control thoughts: Beliefs about the significance of thoughts lead you to feel the need to control your obsessional thoughts (and actions). You worry that, if you don't control (or try to control) unwanted thoughts, something terrible will happen that you could have prevented. Some people worry they will act on their unwanted thoughts unless the thoughts are suppressed.

Intolerance of anxiety: You feel that anxiety or discomfort will persist for ever unless you do something to escape. Sometimes the fear is that the anxiety or emotional discomfort will spiral out of control or lead to 'going crazy', losing control or other harmful consequences.

The **'just right' error (perfectionism):** You feel that things must be 'just right' or perfect in order to be comfortable. A related belief is the feeling that things need to be 'evened out' or symmetrical, or else you will always feel uncomfortable.

Emotional reasoning: You assume that danger is present based simply on the fact that you are feeling anxious.

CHALLENGING YOUR OCD THOUGHTS

Using the thought-challenging techniques outlined in Chapter 5, start to challenge your OCD thoughts. Review the thinking errors above. Can you spot any in your OCD thinking? Do you have any evidence for these? Can you challenge them?

Complete another thought record, using the following headings, and challenge your OCD thinking.

Thinking error	Evidence	How I can challenge it

→ Inflated responsibility in OCD

The more responsible we feel for something, the more likely we are to check that it is safe and secure. The checking feels a relatively small price to pay compared to the imagined consequence of not doing it. The problem for people with OCD is that the original fear becomes lost in a sea of ritualized checking.

Susie's story

'I started checking that my hair straighteners were switched off because I was fearful of burning the house down, but now the issue is that I repeatedly check not only the hair straighteners but every appliance in the house. This takes me about an hour or so to do, so I've started to get up really early before work so that I have time to do this.

'If I've checked all the appliances in a room and then my partner goes into that room, I feel I have to go and check the appliances again, in case he touched something or used something and left it switched on. It's not really fair on him because he should be allowed to use things in his own house, but I can't tolerate it. I find that, if I check everything five times, then I can leave the house, knowing it's OK. Sometimes I replay these checks in my head on the way to work and mentally work my way around the house, checking that all the appliances are off. I guess I'm checking my checking. I've never left anything on.

'I hate staying away from the house because I worry that my partner will leave something plugged in and it will cause a fire. I never used to worry about house fires. My Nan passed away and left me some photos and they're the only ones in the family, so I worry they'd be destroyed. So I guess I check my hair straighteners are off so that I don't destroy the photos and upset my family. I wouldn't cope with that – my mum would be devastated. I couldn't bear to start a fire and for something bad to happen. I can't imagine ever not checking now. I don't know how to stop.'

As you can see from the example above, Susie feels responsible for the protection of her home and the security of some important family photos, and this is making her check a lot more. This highlights the link between responsibility and checking: the more responsibility we feel, the more we feel the need to check:

Responsibility   =   Checking

$\uparrow$ **Responsibility**   = $\uparrow$ **Checking**

CHECKING: WHAT YOU NEED TO KNOW

Checking something more than once leads to uncertainty. This may sound counterintuitive, but doing it more than once actually makes you more uncertain, not less, about whether you have checked something. This is because, when we check something once, our brain stores a clear memory of having checked it, e.g. 'I remember turning the tap off.'

However, OCD introduces doubt into our minds and makes us question whether we have actually checked something or not. This means that we go back and our brain now has to store two incidences of checking, but the second one is full of doubt and so we feel less certain.

This lack of certainty may mean we need to check again, but by this stage our mind is now so full of doubt that we feel uncertain even when we are doing the checking, and so now we have two uncertain memories and one clear memory. Therefore, if you need to check something, *you only need to check it once.*

Checking once is asking for new information for your brain to store and this is perfectly normal. However, checking more than once is simply you seeking reassurance and it serves only to create more confusion and doubt in your brain. You will never learn to relax and trust your memory if you continue to check everything over and over. It's time to reduce your checking.

Exercise 42

REDUCING YOUR CHECKING BEHAVIOUR

In order to reduce your checking behaviour, you first need to identify all the checking you are doing. Don't be embarrassed by having a lot of checks on your list: it is very common for those with OCD to check many different things many times over.

Use the table below to record your checking behaviour. An example has been given to help you get started.

Situation	What did I check?	How did I check it?	How many times did I check it?
Leaving flat to go to work	1 Hall lights were off 2 Bedroom door was shut 3 Kettle was off at the plug	Stared at lights for a count of three Looked at door, looked away, looked back Unplugged kettle and turned switch off	Completed this three times Eight times Unplugged once but went back to check switch was off six times

Now that you have identified all your checking behaviours, go over the list and highlight one or two of the things you check repeatedly.

To reduce your checking, follow this step-by-step plan:

▶ Once you have identified an area of repeated checking, from now on when you are in that area, you may check something only once. For example, in the bathroom, check the taps are off once.

▶ When you have completed your checking, walk away from the area without stopping to check again.

▶ If you feel anxious, try to sit with that anxiety and it will eventually go. If it is too much to bear, put a buffer of a time limit in place, e.g. 'I won't check again for one hour'. Even if you need to go and check again in one hour, you are still breaking the habit of repeated checking on the spot.

▶ Be firm with yourself: you do not need to check more than once. Use the behavioural experiment template outlined in Chapter 6 to help you. What is it you fear will happen if you don't check again? Did it happen? Remember to record your success. Once you have reduced checking in one area, continue to limit your checking in other areas following the same technique. Many people report this being much easier than they thought. This is because it is a firm, strict boundary and OCD responds well to boundaries.

 Don't ask someone to check for you. This is a slippery slope: it is no better than checking yourself because you still believe the situation or thing needs checking and are not giving yourself the opportunity to prove otherwise. If someone has been regularly checking for you, ask them to read the chapter for friends, family and carers (FFC) in this workbook.

ARE YOU *REALLY* RESPONSIBLE FOR THIS?

It is important to consider responsibility carefully and make sure we are not carrying the responsibility of others. In the example of Susie, she could be using the step-by-step plan above to reduce her multiple checking of her hair straighteners, but she also feels responsible for the safety of the house and the photos. Remember that the greater the feeling of responsibility, the greater the OCD symptoms, including checking. Therefore it stands to reason that the less responsibility we feel, the fewer OCD symptoms we will have.

To make sure we carry *only* our responsibility and no one else's, we can use a pie chart to divide up our responsibility. Let's take Susie's example again. Susie's OCD is telling her that everything is *her* responsibility and so her pie chart at the moment would look like this.

My
responsibility

However, let's think about Susie's situation again. Both she and her partner use the appliances in the home, which means that they have shared responsibility for making sure they are switched off or safe to be left on. Manufacturers also have a responsibility to ensure maximum safety for their products. Many products have an automatic shut-off mechanism so they should cut out if they become overheated, and manufacturers bear much of the responsibility for the products' safe use as well. Realistically, therefore, Susie's pie chart should look more like this.

The
manufacturer's
responsibility

My
responsibility

My partner's
responsibility

Yes, Susie does still have some responsibility but only about a third of the amount she originally thought. This means that she can instantly reduce her anxiety down to a third of what it was and then work on overcoming it. It isn't realistic to think that we hold absolute responsibility for absolutely everything – we need to gain a more realistic picture of what our true responsibilities are.

Exercise 43

HOW AM I RESPONSIBLE?

Think of some situations for which you currently feel completely responsible. Now evaluate them honestly and think how you can share that responsibility with others.

Use the pie chart below to help you plot out your responsibility and other people's. If you struggle to do this, ask someone else for their opinion; an objective outsider may be better at seeing a more realistic picture.

Beware of 'scared' OCD – the backlash

As you begin to overcome your OCD, you may notice that it presents you with new fears and ideas that you've never previously thought about. Do not be discouraged by this! This is a good sign – it means that OCD is 'on the run and knows it'. Simply continue to apply the techniques of challenging your thoughts and reducing your checking behviour and you will be able to tackle these new OCD thoughts and behaviour as well.

'Some of your hurts you have cured,
And the sharpest you still have survived,
But what torments of grief you endured
From the evil which never arrived.'

Ralph Waldo Emerson

Summary

1 OCD is a complex anxiety disorder and therefore it cannot be tackled in detail in a single chapter.

2 Remember to separate yourself from your OCD – you didn't ask to have this difficulty and you should not be cross with yourself for the difficulties you face.

3 Do not believe what OCD tells you. Challenge the thoughts and put boundaries in place to contain and limit the impact of the OCD.

What I have learned

→ What are my thoughts, feelings and insights on what I have read so far?

_____

_____

_____

Use the space below to summarize any actions you identify as a result of reading this chapter.

_____

_____

_____

_____

Where to next?

The next chapter focuses on generalized anxiety disorder (GAD). If you don't feel this chapter is going to be relevant or helpful to you, skip ahead to Chapter 11.

10 Working with generalized anxiety disorder (GAD)

In this chapter you will learn:

▶ what generalized anxiety disorder is, its symptoms and how it manifests itself
▶ how to understand and tackle some of your GAD thinking
▶ some practical strategies you can use to help you overcome your GAD.

Generalized anxiety disorder (GAD) refers to a state of anxiety or worry that is excessive, persistent and distressing. This worry is not easily dismissed and as soon as one topic ceases to be a worry a new topic will be found. The term 'generalized' refers to a general state of worrying about most things most of the time and the worry tends to 'float' around from topic to topic.

We all experience anxiety from time to time, and it is common to worry about certain situations as a typical reaction to life events. However, with GAD, one worry simply merges into another, and the level of worry and the depth of worry may be much deeper than for someone else without GAD. People who experience GAD often feel as though they are always worrying, that they cannot relax or enjoy anything without a constant stream of worry running through their mind.

Even if you don't feel you have GAD but you experience ongoing worry, this chapter will be useful for you, to help you identify and overcome some of the worry that you are dealing with.

This chapter is based on the cognitive models of GAD, as outlined by Wells (1995), Freeston & Meares (2008) and Borkovec *et al.* (1983).

> *'Nothing in life is to be feared. It is only to be understood.'*
>
> Marie Curie

Exercise 44

I'M A WORRIER – DO I HAVE GAD?

Many people describe themselves as 'a bit of a worrier' and this doesn't necessarily mean that they are suffering from GAD. As with all anxiety disorders, the key to diagnosis lies in the level of distress and daily interference or disruption caused by the worry.

Look at the diagnostic criteria below and place a tick next to any items that seem familiar to you.

Symptom	Tick
1 Restlessness or feeling keyed up or on edge	
2 Being easily fatigued	
3 Difficulty concentrating or mind going blank	
4 Irritability	
5 Muscle tension	
6 Sleep disturbance (difficulty falling or staying asleep, or restless, unsatisfying sleep)	

If you have been experiencing three or more of these symptoms and they are not related to a specific life event or cannot be explained by another anxiety or other disorder, it may mean that you are being affected by GAD.

If you are experiencing just one or two of these symptoms persistently, the advice in this chapter will still be useful.

The following case study illustrates the way GAD might affect someone and their day-to-day routine.

Sanjay's story

Sanjay has been unable to sleep well for a long time. He finds that, when he goes to bed, his mind will race and, although he tries to relax, he often has to get up in the night to make a note of something he has to do the next day, or check something that will come into his mind when he should be sleeping. Sanjay rarely gets a good night's sleep and worries about the impact this is having on his health.

Sanjay fears that he will get behind at work, although this has never happened, and so he has been working long hours and taking on more responsibility to prove himself at work. However, he now feels that the lack of sleep is making him too tired to function properly and he constantly worries about how he is coming across at work. Sanjay's team can help him with the bigger projects but he worries about looking weak, or as though he can't cope, and so he doesn't use the team. He then worries about looking like a control freak and so tries to give his team the more fun and easy tasks to keep them happy, so that he is working harder and longer hours than anyone else in the office.

After noticing that he has been feeling weak and dizzy and that his heart is racing, he read about his symptoms online and is now worried about the impact on his heart. He went to the doctor to talk about this and was told he was suffering from lack of sleep and was prescribed some sleeping tablets. However, Sanjay worries that, if he was drugged to sleep and an emergency happened, he wouldn't be able to get up and get help, and so he hasn't taken the tablets.

Sanjay had a partner but he continually checked up on him, phoning to ask where he was if he was five minutes late home because he imagined his partner lying dead at the side of the road. The final straw was when Sanjay called the police to report that his partner had been in an accident when, in fact, he had been out with work colleagues.

If his parents don't answer when he makes his regular calls to them, he worries. They have had to give him set times when he can call, to try to control his anxiety, but he often calls throughout the day to check they are OK.

Sanjay reports always being a bit of a worrier and a lot of these worries run 'in the background' of his mind. He has no idea how to stop worrying to get the good night's sleep and relaxation he craves, and he feels that, if he stops worrying about his family, that will make him a bad person.

→ How does GAD start?

We know that worrying about situations or life events is perfectly normal and that many people can go through a period of intense worry in reaction to a stressful event such as redundancy. However, as with a lot of anxieties, these understandable worries can extend to a more generalized anxiety when we experience periods of uncertainty or doubt or are in an unfamiliar situation.

Often these anxieties will grow and we will start to worry about things that we never worried about before. These worries can start from a young age when we experience times of additional stress and anxiety, such as changing schools, taking exams and forming new friendships and relationships. During these periods when so much feels uncertain, we may start worrying about a great many other things too and continue to worry about them excessively. This worrying can become second nature and we may begin to think of ourselves as 'a bit of a worrier' – not questioning the amount we worry.

Indeed, for some people worrying is so much a part of their character that they don't realize just how much they are doing it until something happens to focus them on their worry. Usually the 'something' that happens is an event that causes anxiety and it is almost as though our minds are so full of worry that they literally cannot cope with worrying about anything else. At this point we feel overwhelmed and begin to notice just how worried we have become.

→ How is GAD maintained?

Several factors can maintain GAD and cause us to continue to worry for excessive periods of time, over issues that other people may not worry about or may have fleeting concerns over that are then easily dismissed. One of these factors is the belief about the purpose that worrying serves.

Exercise 45

WHAT DOES WORRYING MEAN TO ME?

In the introduction we briefly looked at the idea that people believe anxiety helps them in some respects, and that it doesn't really affect them in a negative way. Have a look at some of the positive beliefs people hold about their worry in the following table and see which ones you recognize.

Put a tick against the belief about worry that matches yours.

Positive belief about worry	What it means	Is this your belief? (√)
Worry helps me prepare.	People often talk about their worry serving a protective purpose. It is as if the act of worrying somehow prepares us for the worst-case scenario – we are planning ahead for this eventuality. This belief helps us feel more in control as we think ahead to how we would react in a situation.	
Worry makes me a better parent/partner/employee.	When people discuss worrying making them a better person, it is because they believe that worrying shows they care. For example, people believe that, if they worry about their children, they are just being a responsible parent and that it shows how much they love their children.	
If I worry, I can prevent bad things happening as God/fate/destiny will not interfere.	This belief often links to one around external control, with people believing that, if they worry, then God/fate/destiny will see that they care and have thought about something and so nothing bad will happen.	
Worry keeps me going.	People often believe that a little bit of worry and stress keeps them going and motivated, so that they achieve more: an individual may believe that worrying about losing their job ensures that they work harder and achieve more at work.	
Worry keeps me one step ahead.	This belief highlights how people feel that worrying gives them the edge. They are already one step ahead of life events and have prepared for several different scenarios and so are ready for anything. This sense of being prepared for day-to-day life can also help us feel a lot more in control.	

From the list above you may have recognized some positive beliefs you hold about your own worry. You may also have thought of some other positive beliefs that you have about worry and the role it plays in your own life.

Use the space below to list any additional positive beliefs about your worry that were not listed above.

_____

_____

_____

_____

_____

_____

As well as positive beliefs about worry, it is possible for people to worry about worry. Have a look at the thoughts about worrying in the table below and tick any that you recognize as yours.

Negative belief about worry	What it means	Is this your belief? (√)
Worry is making me ill.	Anxiety can have a strong physical effect on us, causing anything from tension headaches, upset stomachs and nausea to an overall feeling of shakiness and trembling or physical weakness. This can cause us to worry that our anxieties are causing us genuine physical harm.	
Worry is driving me mad.	The nature of worrying means that we often experience our minds racing. It seems as if we cannot control our thoughts; when we try to relax, our mind instead fills with worries and makes us feel on edge and unable to relax. This can make us feel completely out of control of our own minds and can even leave us feeling we are 'going mad' or 'losing the plot'.	

Negative belief about worry	What it means	Is this your belief? (√)
I'm making other people worry.	This belief can have two meanings. Sometimes we feel so anxious and uptight that we think other people must also be worrying about us and our anxieties. This may happen if we involve other people in our worry, e.g. by asking them for reassurance so they know when we are worrying. The other belief is that somehow we are passing our worry on and this causes us to give other people things to worry about, e.g. you telling a partner you are worried about him driving home may lead him to worry about his journey and become anxious about driving, which he never has been anxious about before.	
Worry means there is something wrong with me.	The act of constantly worrying can make us feel completely overwhelmed with thoughts of worst-case scenarios and hypothetical disasters that may or may not occur. This can lead us to believe that there is something fundamentally wrong with us. We may believe we are weak in some way or incapable of coping as well as other people. This belief can then reduce our confidence and our faith in ourselves that we can cope and may lead to further worrying.	
I don't know how to stop worrying.	People often believe that they cannot stop worrying. As it can feel so difficult to stop worrying thoughts coming into your mind, and to dismiss them when they do come in, people often feel trapped in a worry cycle. This means that they believe they will never be able to stop worrying and will simply continue to worry about everything for evermore. (NB: This isn't the case – worry and anxiety are treatable conditions, but it is easy to see how this belief develops, given the relentless and persistent nature of anxiety.)	

This list of worries about worry will have allowed you to identify some of your own worries about worry. Use the space below to write down any other worries about worry that you experience.

_____

_____

_____

_____

_____

_____

· ·

Recognizing the beliefs we hold about worry is useful for showing us why we continue to worry. Having recognized your beliefs, it is important to start challenging the role that worry plays in your life. In order to do this, you need to understand that the beliefs are based in fear, not fact, and that the beliefs may actually be making you worry even more.

 Exercise 46

 ## OVERCOMING THE ANXIETY

To help you challenge your beliefs, here are some questions about the positive beliefs listed in the previous exercise. Focus on each belief and use the questions to challenge it, seeing it as affecting and maintaining your worry rather than helping you to stop worrying.

Consider the beliefs listed in the following table and answer the questions designed to challenge them.

Belief about worry	Questions to help you challenge this belief
Worry helps me prepare.	• When you worry, are you able to make clear and concise plans? Or does your mind simply race around worst-case scenarios? • Do you need to spend your time preparing for scenarios that might never happen? • Would your energy not be better spent preparing for scenarios which you know will happen, and things you want to achieve, than for eventualities that may never occur? • Does worry really help you feel any more prepared?
Worry makes me a better parent/partner/employee.	• Des the act of worrying really make you a better person and show you care? • Is it possible that, while you are spending so much time worrying, you are not paying attention to what is actually happening and therefore might miss something important at work/home/school? • While meaning to be more careful, does worrying in fact make you distracted and forgetful? • Does worrying make you feel so overwhelmed that you cannot cope?
If I worry, I can prevent bad things happening as God/fate/destiny will not interfere.	• Do you really hold any power over any of these things? • Do you really believe that God/fate/destiny is malevolent and will punish you unless you worry about these things considerably? • Do you have any evidence that this is the case?
Worry keeps me going.	• Can you be motivated without worrying? • Wouldn't more confidence in yourself be a better motivator than fear of failure? • Have you any evidence that says you cannot succeed without worrying? • Is it possible that worrying so much means you miss out on bigger opportunities because you are too bogged down in worrying? • Does worry push you or hinder you?
Worry keeps me one step ahead.	• Do you need to worry to be prepared for the day ahead? • Do other people worry excessively in order to prepare for the day ahead? (If not, what do they do instead?) • Do you need to worry to prepare? • Wouldn't you feel more energized, confident and relaxed for the day ahead if you could stop worrying?

Now add your own questions and answers below: as before, use the space to challenge any additional beliefs about worry that you know you hold.

_____

_____

_____

_____

_____

You have now challenged some of the positive beliefs you held about your anxiety, and you can do the same with your negative beliefs. Review your answers and consider how much you still believe in the benefit of worrying.

This challenging will show you that, although anxiety is a horrible experience and constant worry can impact on your well-being and daily life and limit your future, it is not dangerous in itself. However, it is unpleasant, so the sooner we take control back from the worry, the better.

→ Record and classify your anxiety

Now that we have identified the role that worry itself plays, it is helpful to consider *what* you are actually worrying about. As already mentioned, those with and without anxiety will worry about the same things. However, those with GAD are more likely to worry excessively about 'hypothetical' situations or worries than those without GAD.

REAL AND HYPOTHETICAL WORRIES

Real worries are worries about current problems or real events that we may be able to solve or over which we may be able to exert some control. These may include worries such as:

▶ 'Have I got enough money to pay this month's gas bill?'

▶ 'Lucy has been quiet recently. What if something's wrong?'

▶ 'What if I muck up that presentation at work?'

Hypothetical worries are worries about things which have not happened and over which you have almost no control. These may include worries such as:

▶ 'What if the plane crashes when I go on holiday?'
▶ 'What if I get cancer?'
▶ 'What if I lose my job?'

Sometimes real worries can spiral out of control into hypothetical worries. For example:

▶ 'My train is delayed; what if I'm late for work?' – real worry
▶ 'If I'm late for work, I'll miss an important office announcement.' hypothetical worry
▶ 'Maybe the announcement will be about job cuts and I'll miss out by not knowing what's going on.' – hypothetical worry
▶ 'Maybe I'll be fired, and I'll have no money and will be homeless.' hypothetical worry

As you can see, hypothetical worries can spiral out of very typical real worries. It is fairly typical to be concerned that you might be late for work if your train is delayed. It is not typical, however, to then go on to worry about being homeless.

Exercise 47

ARE MY WORRIES REAL?

In the following table, write down your typical worries in a day and then use the right-hand column to decide whether these are real or hypothetical worries. An example of each type of worry has been included to help you.

Situation	Worry	Real or hypothetical?
Driving to work and getting caught in traffic	I might be late for work if this traffic gets any worse.	Real
Driving to work and getting caught in traffic	Paul left the house before me this morning; maybe he had an accident on this road and that's what is causing the traffic.	Hypothetical

Now that you have identified the types of worry that you experience, and your own beliefs about the purpose of worry, we are going to examine some strategies and skills you can use to help you overcome this worry.

→ Problem-solving

While worrying about something can make us feel as though we are preparing ourselves and therefore doing something useful, worrying rarely serves any practical purpose. In fact, we can spend so much time worrying that we forget to come to any conclusion or reach a solution. When dealing with real worries, it is therefore important to try to problem-solve some of them, in order to reduce the anxiety they cause and help the situation feel more under control.

HOW DO I PROBLEM-SOLVE?

Problem-solving is a practical approach to dealing with worries and it gives us a hands-on solution to help the situation rather than just sitting and worrying about it. An easy way to know whether you are problem-solving or merely worrying about something is to ask yourself whether you have come up with a solution or are just repeating the same worry over and over.

Stage 1

Check that this is a real worry. Using the skill you learned above, check whether the worry is real or hypothetical. Because hypothetical worries are about situations that don't exist, we cannot problem-solve them.

Stage 2

Take the emotion out of the worry. Rather than thinking about the emotional consequence or burden of a problem (e.g. how embarrassed you would be if you couldn't pay your credit card bill), instead describe the problem in practical terms. You should try to summarize your problem in one or two sentences – this will force you to be brief and succinct and therefore stick to the facts of the problem only.

Stage 3

Break the problem down into small steps. Make these as small as they need to be in order to feel manageable; it doesn't matter how many steps there are.

Stage 4

Start tackling the problems one by one. The temptation with things that worry us is to put them off, but all this does is delay the inevitable and give us plenty of time for anxiety to breed. As anxiety becomes greater and greater, it can begin to feel easier to put off facing a problem and tackling it (think back to the cycle of avoidance). Therefore it is better to confront something as soon as possible, as soon as the worry starts.

TAKE BACK CONTROL – PUT WORRY ON THE SPOT

Anxiety and worries can force themselves into our thoughts when we are trying to focus and concentrate on other things. This leads to distraction and distress, and a feeling of having no control over our own minds.

Anxiety responds very well to boundaries and discipline. As it is such a chaotic messy beast, it needs boundaries to contain it and keep it under control. This is where a technique called a 'worry spot' comes in.

The principle of a worry spot is that you decide when and where you are going to worry. You choose a time of day when you are going to focus solely on the worry and not do anything else. This may sound contradictory to your goal of trying to reduce worry, but by doing this you will find that you worry less. This is because you decide when you will worry.

For example, let's say you decide your worry spot is going to be at 3 p.m. every day and at that time you are going to worry solidly for 20 minutes. Until 3 p.m., every time a worry comes into your head you will tell it to go away. It may sound simple, but the basis of this suits anxiety well because you are not ignoring or suppressing the worry but taking control of it.

 Do not choose a time near bedtime because it can be harder to switch off if you have been worrying just before bed and then have nothing to do in order to distract you. For the same reason, don't take your worry to your bedroom if you can avoid it. You want to do your worrying somewhere separate from where you sleep and relax if possible.

Exercise 48

 ## THE WORRY SPOT TECHNIQUE

Sit down and work out when is going to be a good time for you to worry. In order to help you identify a good worry spot, answer the questions below:

▶ When are you least likely to be disturbed?

▶ When can you have enough time to sit and worry without having to dash off or do other things?

▶ Where are you going to worry?

▶ How are you going to protect the time? (e.g. saying to a partner or colleague, 'I'm going to be busy for the next 20 minutes and cannot be disturbed.')

Once you have identified a good worry spot for you, make a note of it, put it in your calendar or diary, or set an alarm on your phone. Use the space below to make a note of your chosen worry spot.

→ My worry spot will take place on:_____

→ Time of day?_____

→ Where?_____

→ For how long?_____

Write down your worries in the space below if you need to. This may seem unnecessary but, approaching a worry spot, you may begin to worry that you will forget your worries (ironic, I know) and forget to worry about something important.

_____

_____

_____

_____

_____

_____

To complete a successful worry spot, take yourself to your chosen spot where you won't be disturbed. Now deliberately make yourself worry about the things you normally worry about and anything else that has popped into your head throughout the day up to this point or since your last worry spot.

It is common to feel emotional when you are deliberately worrying, not least because you are thinking about things that you normally try to avoid worrying about. However, you will find that you are better able to contain your worry and that worrying for 20–30 minutes a day under your own control is a lot more manageable than worrying non-stop.

Using a worry spot will help you feel as though you are regaining control over your mind and this will help limit your worries. After using worry spots for a while, you will find that your anxiety naturally subsides very quickly and that you may need to use the worry spots less and less, maybe only once a week or even once a month. Imagine worrying for only 20 minutes a month instead of constantly!

Top tips for successful worrying

- Set a timer.

- It's easy to become distracted by your worry and therefore lose track of time. Set a timer for 20–30 minutes in order to avoid running over your allotted time.

- Move.

- Once you have finished your worry spot, move around and start doing something different. Get up from the chair, go to a different room, or make yourself a cuppa. By getting up and immediately doing something different, you are giving your body and mind a physical cue that the worry spot is over and it's time to focus on something else.

- Split the time.

- If one worry spot doesn't feel enough and you find it difficult to contain your worries, simply split the worry spot into two spots of 10–15 minutes each. You are still only worrying for 20–30 minutes, but doing it this way may make it more manageable.

- Write down your worries.

- Keeping a list of things to worry about during your worry spots will help you feel as though you have covered your worries and you won't forget anything.

- Reward yourself.

- Making yourself worry can feel quite draining at first because worrying is exhausting. Try to plan to do something nice after your worry spot, even if it is a small reward – this will help you feel motivated to continue.

'The only thing we have to fear is fear itself.'

Franklin D. Roosevelt

Summary

1 In order to stop worrying, you need to challenge your beliefs about the purpose of worry.

2 Instead of worrying, do some problem-solving and tackle the situation. You will feel better and calmer for doing something practical and the worry will naturally diminish as a result.

3 Take control of when you worry by using a 'worry spot'.

What I have learned

→ What are my thoughts, feelings and insights on what I have read so far?

_____

_____

_____

Use the space below to summarize any actions you identify as a result of reading this chapter.

_____

_____

_____

Where to next?

This chapter is the final one of the four that look at specific anxiety disorders. The next chapter focuses on tips for friends, family and carers (FFC), looking at the skills and strategies that those around you can use to help you manage and overcome your anxiety.

11

How friends, family and carers can help

● ●

In this chapter you will learn:

▶ why someone might have anxiety or an anxiety disorder

▶ how you can support a person with anxiety by separating the person from the anxiety

▶ how to limit behaviour which may have been maintaining their anxiety.

● ●

Living with, working with or even spending time with someone with anxiety can be stressful. This is because anxiety is complex and all-encompassing and it can be difficult to know what to do when someone you care about is feeling anxious.

This chapter contains exercises for you to complete, but the main focus is on offering an explanation of anxiety as well as some shared experiences of friends, family and carers who have lived with someone with anxiety.

> '*My life has been full of terrible misfortunes –*
> *most of which have never happened.*'
>
> Michel de Montaigne

→ Why are they anxious?

Trying to understand why someone is feeling anxious can be difficult, particularly if you are in the same situation as they are but not experiencing anxiety. This can lead us to question why they worry or feel anxious about things that we don't. What is it about us – or them – that means they are feeling anxiety where we are not?

It can be difficult to understand another person's anxiety, and sometimes the person themselves will be unable to pinpoint exactly why they feel anxious; they will just know that they do. This can make it even harder to try to understand why someone is feeling anxious.

However, what is important to realize is that anxiety, like low mood, can happen to anyone. Anxiety and depression are the 'common colds of the mind' and they do not discriminate. Anxiety can affect anyone, no matter what their circumstances. Anxiety is not personal. It is not something that they have done or are doing that is making someone anxious, nor does it mean that they are unhappy in some way.

However, when someone feels anxious, it means they are worried about something, and this worry can often be related to or grow out of fears and anxieties that developed many years ago, maybe even before you knew this person. The key message here is that anxiety is no one's fault.

ANXIETY'S BY-PRODUCTS: GUILT, BLAME AND SHAME

It is common for those who experience anxiety to be very self-critical. You may hear the person you know with anxiety describe themselves in a critical way, saying things like:

▶ 'I'm such an idiot.

▶ 'Everyone else copes – why don't I?'

▶ 'There are people far worse off than I am – why am I worrying about things so much when other people have much worse things to worry about?'

Because this self-critical language reflects what those with anxiety are thinking about themselves, people who feel very anxious may also start to feel quite low in mood. You may notice that the person you care about starts to experience symptoms of depression along with their anxiety.

ARE THEY DEPRESSED?

Look at the checklist of depressive symptoms below and tick any that apply to the person you know who is feeling anxious. The more you tick, the more likely it is that they are feeling low; with mostly ticks, the more severe the symptoms of depression will be.

Symptoms	Tick
Feeling depressed or low for most of the day	
Loss of pleasure in activities/things previously enjoyed	
Significant weight loss or weight gain	
Disruption to sleep pattern – sleeping a lot more or less than usual	
Feeling fatigued or lacking in energy most days	
Feeling worthless or guilty for no obvious reason most of the time	
Difficulties with memory and concentration	
Difficulty 'getting going' in the morning – wanting to stay in bed	
Feeling overwhelmed	
No longer interested in appearance, e.g. not combing hair/wearing make-up	
Reduced social interaction/not seeing other people as much as before	
Thoughts of suicide or being better off dead	

If someone you know is exhibiting the symptoms above, particularly if they have mentioned suicidal thoughts or ideas, they will need help. You should encourage them to contact their GP as soon as possible in order to be referred for support.

Sometimes, if people are feeling low, it is much harder for them to seek help for, and work on, their anxiety, This is because, when we feel very depressed, we lose interest in activities and doing things and we care less about ourselves. This means we may need more support or motivation in order to seek treatment. If someone you know is struggling to motivate themselves, perhaps you can offer to go with them to an appointment. Explain to that person that low mood and anxiety very often go together and the way they are feeling is therefore very common.

However, both anxiety and depression are eminently treatable conditions and therefore it is important to get help as soon as possible so that the person can stop experiencing these feelings and start to enjoy their life again.

→ This is not the person I used to know

Anxiety can seem to completely engulf the person you know and replace them with a nervous wreck who cannot stop worrying. This can be distressing for many reasons, not least because anxiety is unpleasant, and you watch someone you care about experience this. Anxiety can get in the way of social occasions and/or work, which can place a strain on a friendship or relationship.

You can help to deal with that person's anxiety in several ways. Firstly, separate out the anxiety from the person. Anxiety is a bully: a horrible, messy, chaotic bully. Although it may feel as though someone permanently anxious has replaced the person you care about, the person you care about is still there. It is just that they are underneath this big bully, which is anxiety.

Start to separate out these experiences from the person you care about. Start to notice when the person makes a decision as opposed to when anxiety makes a decision. People talk about how their marriage, partnership or friendship has become crowded by the anxiety and that's because it is as though a third and very unwelcome person has moved into the household. This unwelcome visitor is anxiety and it can seem to dominate everything. However, do not worry. Anxiety is a short-stay guest and you can help kick it out of your household, no matter how strong it feels at times.

 *Exercise 50*

 THE PERSON OR THE ANXIETY?

To start noticing the difference between the anxiety and the person you care about, use the chart below to observe the person for a week or so and notice when you feel they are present and making decisions and when you feel it is their anxiety doing so. A couple of examples have been included to help you.

Situation	When were they present?	When was their anxiety present?
Going to a friend's house for a barbecue	Sitting on the grass laughing with some of our friends, playing with the children	On the way home, she kept asking about people looking at her and whether she had offended someone who left early, even though it was nothing to do with her and she hadn't said or done anything wrong.
Leaving for work this morning	Over breakfast, chatting about a news story on the radio	Couldn't find car keys – shouted at me that I had moved them, even though I hadn't touched them. Eventually found them in his jacket but by then he was saying he was going to be late and was very stressed and grumpy. Not a nice start to the day.

Exercise 51

HOW DOES THEIR ANXIETY AFFECT US?

'I get so angry and fed up with them and then I feel bad – after all, it's not their fault.'

This is a very common experience among carers, family members and friends of those dealing with anxiety.

It's important to recognize the impact that someone else's anxiety is having on you. Have a look at the statements below, which relate to the ways anxiety can affect us and interfere in our lives.

Read the statements and tick the ones you agree with.

Statement	Tick
I don't talk to them as much as I used to.	
I don't share my problems with them because I don't want to worry them.	
I take on more responsibility than I used to.	
I do more than my fair share around the house/at work/with day-to-day tasks because they cannot cope.	
I have to deal with a lot more, e.g. family circumstances and events, life events, illness, on my own.	
I don't feel supported any more.	
I feel my role has changed from friend/partner/spouse/colleague to one of carer.	
They shout at me a lot more/we have more arguments than we used to.	
I do more/put up with a lot for an easy life.	
I don't recognize the person they have become/anxiety has changed them.	
They constantly need reassurance and will interrupt what I am doing in order for me to reassure them, e.g. eating, working, sleeping.	
I find myself worrying about things alone so as not to add to their list of anxieties.	
I feel I carry more burdens than they do as I try not to give them anything else to deal with.	
When they are feeling anxious, they withdraw. It doesn't matter what I am saying or doing, they are not really in the moment with me.	
I am exhausted by their anxiety.	
I have to deal with all the finances and bills in our household/at work because they can't.	

Use the space below to write down your own experiences of and reactions to someone else's anxiety that may not have been included in the above statements.

_____

_____

_____

_____

_____

_____

_____

_____

_____

Now remove yourself from the situation and imagine a friend is telling you that they have been experiencing some of the above. Wouldn't you think they were entitled to feel angry or fed up? Whether the person can help it or not, being put in these situations is exhausting, frustrating and distressing and it is important to recognize that.

Thinking back to the previous exercise, where you separated out the person with anxiety from the anxiety itself, you will realize what anxiety is doing in these situations. It is not the person you are angry at, but rather their anxiety. It is not them you are fed up with, but you _are_ fed up with dealing with their anxiety.

By separating the two things out and understanding that it is absolutely normal and reasonable to be fed up with that person's anxiety, you can get rid of some of the guilt and blame you put on yourself.

It is OK to be angry with anxiety. Just recognize that it is the anxiety you are angry at and not the person with the anxiety. This can be an important message to share with the person who is anxious because they will be worried about your reaction and how you are feeling.

→ Why reassurance doesn't work

'I constantly tell them they've nothing to worry about but it doesn't seem to stop them worrying. How can I get through to them?'

Being asked to reassure someone is a common experience for those close to someone with anxiety. We can be asked for, and offer, reassurance in many different ways, sometimes without even realizing we are reassuring someone. For example, if you are always the last person to leave the house, this may just be coincidence. However, it may be that you are offering some reassurance about the house being locked securely or that everything is turned off. It may not even be that the person with anxiety realizes they are doing this, but sometimes it is as though they are giving you the responsibility and then can reassure themselves that, if anything goes wrong, it is your fault. Charming!

However we offer reassurance, either by answering direct questions or checking something for someone, what you will notice is that the reassurance doesn't work. If reassurance worked, we would never be anxious, and there'd be no need for this book.

The reason reassurance doesn't work is because it can actually feed anxiety in many different ways. Although, initially, the person may feel less anxious, very quickly the anxiety will creep back in and they will feel increasingly anxious and need further reassurance, and so on. This is a vicious cycle to get caught up in because, once you reassure, it is very hard to stop reassuring, as you may well have discovered.

HOW REASSURANCE LEADS TO PROBLEMS

The process of offering reassurance goes against the principles of CBT therapy, which are about challenging the anxious thoughts and discovering for ourselves what happens when we go through a situation. The case study below describes a situation involving an anxious child and her parents and highlights the role reassurance played in maintaining the child's anxiety.

Lucy's story

Lucy, aged 10, had a bad dream one night. She dreamed that she left her bedroom window open and a ghost slipped through it and into her parents' room, where it killed them both. Following this dream, Lucy became very scared of going to bed.

The next night she asked her parents to check that both her bedroom windows were closed and that nothing could get in. Lucy's parents checked the windows for her and offered her the reassurance that the windows were closed and that no baddies or ghosts could get through. Lucy thought to herself, 'I'm right to worry because, if the ghost wasn't real, they wouldn't also be worried about the ghost and wouldn't be checking my window.'

Lucy then became worried about other windows in the house and wouldn't go to bed until she had walked around the house with both her parents, checking that all the windows were closed. When Lucy's parents became frustrated by this, particularly in warm weather, Lucy cried and screamed until they had checked the windows with her.

Lucy's parents didn't like seeing her so distressed and it seemed a small task to do, so they continued to check all the windows with Lucy every night before bed. This meant that Lucy's parents could not go out for the evening or, if they did, they needed to be back in time to check the windows with Lucy.

Three things are noticeable from this case study:

1 You can understand why Lucy thinks there is a real threat. After all, if there were nothing to worry about, her parents wouldn't check, would they? What Lucy doesn't understand is that they are checking to reassure her, not because there is a real threat from any ghost.

2 You can see why Lucy's parents are offering her this reassurance. To witness the distress of someone we care about is heartbreaking, and it seems a small task to complete to keep them calm and alleviate some of their anxiety.

3 We can see just how quickly reassurance seeking grows until it is out of control. You start by offering a small reassurance, which is very quick to do, but it soon grows into a task and then into a whole routine. Fear of ghosts is no longer the problem: the problem is now the elaborate checking ritual that Lucy and her parents have developed to help reduce her anxiety.

WHAT TO DO INSTEAD OF REASSURING

Instead of using reassurance, we need to help the person challenge their fears and anxiety-driven beliefs. Had Lucy been in therapy, what Lucy's parents would have been doing is flinging her bedroom windows wide open and then going to bed. That way, in the morning, when they hadn't been killed, Lucy would have realized that there was nothing to worry about. Even though those initial few nights would have been scary for Lucy, very quickly she would have become confident that there was no threat to her parents.

Equally, when Lucy had the anxiety about the ghost she had dreamed of, she would have had real evidence to counter this anxious belief. This would have dramatically reduced the impact until she stopped having the anxiety altogether.

Therefore, in CBT we do not try to offer specific reassurance. Instead, we are trying to give the person an opportunity to challenge their thoughts. This is a very different approach – and one that quashes anxiety once and for all.

Exercise 52

HOW AM I REASSURING?

Think about the level of reassurance you are offering on a daily basis. Notice the different ways you may be offering reassurance, from checking something for someone or telling them directly not to worry and that everything is fine, or maybe answering a direct question that someone is asking you when they are anxious.

Use the table below to note your thoughts, with the example as a guide to help you.

Situation	Reassurance offered
Partner cooking and becomes anxious about leaving the gas on	I took over the cooking so that I was the last one to use the oven. I checked the gas was off myself and, when they asked me if it was off, I said 'Yes'. When watching TV, partner asked me again if the gas was off and I said 'Yes'. They said 'Are you sure?' I said 'Yes'. They were noticeably distressed, so I got up and checked that the gas was off again and then came back and told them it was definitely off. My partner then relaxed.

HOW TO STOP REASSURING

As we can see from the case of Lucy, it is easy to get caught up in a cycle of reassurance and it can become part of our daily routine. However, reassurance can be much harder to stop and you may want to try one of the strategies below to help you.

▶ **Explain why you are no longer reassuring.**

Explain to the person with anxiety that you realize that reassurance makes it worse and so you are going to help support them to overcome their anxiety instead of offering reassurance.

▶ **If you cannot stop straight away, start to limit your reassurance.**

Sometimes it can be hard immediately to stop the reassurance you have been giving and so instead you may want to start reducing the amount. Maybe limit yourself to offering three reassurances per day and then the person with anxiety will have to choose when they need reassurance the most. Be sure to tell them you are doing this and don't be tempted to offer more reassurance. This may feel cruel, but remember: reassurance only feeds the anxiety and makes it worse.

▶ **If I don't reassure them, they become angry and we argue.**

Anxiety can make us behave irrationally and we can snap and shout at people, even if we are very close to them and care about them. Ask yourself, 'Would I put up with this if the anxiety wasn't an issue?' If the answer is no, then don't tolerate the behaviour.

> *'Worry often gives a small thing a big shadow.'*
>
> Swedish proverb

Summary

1 Trying to understand why someone is feeling anxious can be difficult, particularly if you are in the same situation as they are but not experiencing anxiety yourself.

2 Anxiety and depression are the 'common colds of the mind'. Anxiety does not discriminate: it can affect anyone, no matter what their circumstances.

3 Separating the person from their anxiety, and recognizing that it is absolutely normal and reasonable to be fed up and angry with that person's anxiety, will help you get rid of some of the guilt and blame you put on yourself. It is ok to be angry with anxiety.

4 Reassurance does not help anxiety in the long term. Although it may provide short-term relief, ultimately it only feeds the anxiety and is not helpful for someone trying to overcome their anxiety.

What I have learned

→ What are my thoughts, feelings and insights on what I have read so far?

_____

_____

_____

Use the space below to summarize any actions you identify as a result of reading this chapter.

_____

_____

_____

Where to next?

The next chapter focuses on how to adjust to living life without anxiety and how to prevent a relapse.

12 Enjoying life without anxiety: relapse prevention

In this chapter you will learn:

▶ what life can be like after recovery from anxiety
▶ what might get in the way of living 'anxiety free'
▶ some relapse-prevention strategies to help you manage any future anxiety.

If you have always been a worrier, it can be difficult to imagine a future without anxiety. Being someone who worries can become a big part of our identity and it can take up a lot of our time. This means that, when the worry and anxiety stop, we can be left feeling unsure of what to do with ourselves.

Once you have overcome and taken control back over your anxiety, it is important to establish who you are without it. Anxiety gets in the way of many things, such as spontaneity and fun, and it can prevent us from taking advantage of opportunities. If this has been the case for you, now is the time to re-establish who you are and uncover your own identity again.

> *'Many of our fears are tissue-paper-thin, and a single courageous step would carry us clear through them.'*
>
> Brendan Francis

WHO WAS I THEN?

Think of a time before you were anxious. What were you like? What did you enjoy doing? What was different about you then? Try to remember who you were without anxiety and who you would like to get back to being, as this will help direct you for your future.

Write down the top ten things that anxiety has prevented you from doing that you've always wanted to do. Then turn them into your to-do list (remember your SMART goal principles here).

→ My top ten anxiety-free to-do list:

1_____

2_____

3_____

4_____

5_____

6_____

7_____

8_____

9_____

10_____

Keep future focused

What else is possible now that your anxiety is under control? What else can you do in the future that you never thought possible? Remember, it wasn't you saying that you couldn't do these things – it was your anxiety. Take real pleasure in proving that anxiety was wrong!

→ Common lingering worries

People often have the following questions about becoming anxiety free:

▶ **If I stop worrying, does that mean I stop caring?**

No. As discussed throughout this book, we have all sorts of unhelpful beliefs about the purpose of worry but worrying and caring about something are not the same thing. Remember to challenge those beliefs about worry and the purpose it serves.

▶ **Who will worry about the things I used to worry about?**

We can consider ourselves to be 'stuck' in a role. For example, if we are the person who always worries about things, we become known as 'the worrier' and other people can leave all that worrying to us. Although we may feel stuck in our roles, in fact everyone's role is fluid and, if one person shifts in role, then others will also shift to accommodate this change.

Use a behavioural experiment to test out what happens if you adopt a different role and act differently in a situation. The key is to communicate what your needs are, rather than just worrying about everyone else's.

→ The new you in old relationships

It can feel quite daunting and difficult to introduce the new 'anxiety-free' you to people who have known you be anxious for a while. Often we feel completely different without anxiety and capable of doing or saying things that anxiety has prevented us from doing. However, even if someone has been following your journey out of anxiety, it can still be difficult for them to understand the new, changed you.

Take the following steps to help you and those around you adapt to the new you and overcome any lingering barriers to overcoming your anxiety.

1 BE CLEAR ON WHAT HAS CHANGED

The first step to introducing people to the new you is to be clear about what has changed and what you now expect from them. This is extremely important because, while we feel very different on the inside, very little will have changed on the outside and, as we know, people are not mind readers. Therefore they may be completely unaware of how differently you are feeling.

 *Exercise 54*

 IDENTIFYING WHAT HAS CHANGED

Think about someone you are in a relationship with, whether it's a friendship, a working relationship or a romantic relationship. Now consider some of the things that may have changed for you in this relationship as a result of you tackling your anxiety.

Complete the table below to help you summarize this information. Use the example as a guide to help you.

Relationship: Partner	
When I was anxious…	Now I am not anxious
she used to check things for me	I know it is unhelpful and so want to check things myself.

2 SHARE THE INFORMATION

Although it can feel exposing, it is important to share the information you have identified above with others. Ask someone to spend some time with you going through the list and highlighting the changes you have made and how you would like things to be different.

3 HELP THEM ACCEPT THE NEW YOU

Sometimes we can feel as if we are a completely different person without anxiety and the changes we want to make can feel extreme. If your partner, friend or colleague is finding it difficult to accept the new you, try to have a conversation together, asking them to name some of their concerns or reluctance.

Some of the most common difficulties people face are listed below. If you get stuck in your conversation, use these as prompts to guide you. Ask the person you are in a relationship with to look at the list and highlight any reasons that are true for them.

▶ 'We've been here before.'

Sometimes, if you have made progress before but then felt anxious again, it can be difficult for people to feel that the changes now are different or more permanent.

▶ 'I don't know how much to help.'

It may be that your partner/friend/colleague has become used to doing everything for you and the idea of handing that responsibility back may feel too much for them. They may be worried about how much to help, and about overwhelming you or making you feel worse.

▶ 'What do I do if you get anxious again?'

Many people don't know what to do for the best when someone they care about is feeling anxious and they worry about making the situation worse.

▶ 'I can't trust you any more.'

It is hard to hear this, but sometimes people can feel that they have had to take on extra responsibility or handle situations that you have been unable to manage when anxious. This means they can feel that they are the only person who can handle them. When we were anxious, we may also have broken promises or been unable to complete tasks when our anxiety became too much to cope with. This means that others may find it difficult to trust that we can do something when we say we feel better now.

 *Exercise 55*

 ## OVERCOMING THE BARRIERS

Now that you have identified the barriers that get in the way, the key is to keep discussing them. Tell someone what you would like to achieve, where you think you might need help and support and what you anticipate their role to be.

List your thoughts in the spaces below (an example for each item has been given as a guide to help you).

→ I would like to:

(e.g. complete the weekly shop on my own)

_____

_____

_____

_____

_____

_____

→ I might need help with:

(e.g. a bit of encouragement)

_____

_____

_____

_____

_____

→ I would like you to:

(e.g. remind me that I can do it and to challenge my anxious beliefs. *Do not* offer to go instead of me; this is something I need to do)

_____

_____

_____

_____

By being open and honest about what you hope to achieve and what you would and wouldn't like help with, you are helping someone else understand how you are feeling and what they can do to support you. This should make things a lot clearer and it will then be easier for them to adapt to your new way of being.

→ Beware old habits

When you first start overcoming your anxiety, you may catch yourself making thinking errors or starting to become anxious before you apply the techniques that you have learned throughout this book. This is because your mind will have formed a habit of anxious thinking and so it will automatically start to think anxious thoughts about a situation.

If this happens to you, be nice to yourself. There is no point adding criticism and guilt to your feelings of anxiety. Instead, just acknowledge that it will take a bit of time to break the habit and then apply one or more of the techniques learned to help reduce your anxiety. To begin with, you will need to make a conscious effort to retrain your thinking to new paths that are logical and evidence-based, not anxiety-based. However, after a very short time, your brain will form new thinking habits that will become automatic.

→ Review your goals

It is important continually to review your goals, as this can act as motivation. It can also help you recognize areas where anxiety may have crept back in and be holding you back without you realizing it.

Ask yourself what's more important: keeping anxiety happy or doing what you want to do? Would you want 'worried to death' written on your tombstone? Checking in with your goals and what you have and haven't achieved keeps you on track and means you keep challenging your anxiety.

Exercise 56

REVIEWING YOUR GOALS

Review your goals, considering the following questions.

→ What have I achieved so far?

_____

_____

_____

_____

→ What is left to achieve?

_____

_____

_____

_____

→ How can I use the techniques learned to help me achieve my next goals?

_____

_____

_____

_____

Continue to review your goals on a regular basis and watch out for any areas where anxiety might be holding you back. Identify new goals and challenges for yourself for the future, to help you stay focused.

→ What if my anxiety comes back?

One of the things that can hold us back is the fear of our anxiety and worry returning. Sometimes we are nervous about trying anything new or challenging ourselves, in case the anxiety comes back and we feel overwhelmed again. If this is you, then remember the following key points

▶ **This is an anxious belief.**

The worry about anxiety coming back if you push yourself 'too far' is an anxiety-driven belief – so challenge it! Push yourself further and see what happens. This way, you continue to challenge the anxiety and you'll find out just how much you *are* capable of, rather than being dictated to by the anxiety.

▶ **You never go back to square one.**

The idea of going back to square one can feel very intimidating but it's important to remember that you *never* go back to square one. Now you know what a liar anxiety is, how it affects you and the strategies to overcome it, you are in a much better position than you were before. You are better equipped, stronger and more confident than you were before you started tackling anxiety. You may experience a relapse, but you will never go back to square one.

▶ **You can take steps to prevent a relapse.**

The next part of this chapter focuses on relapse prevention. It will help you plan for any setbacks and allow you to develop a clear 'blueprint' or plan for what to do in case this happens.

→ Relapse prevention

It is never possible to live life *completely* free from anxiety. Life events will occur that cause us to have understandable feelings of anxiety and worry. If, however, you feel as though your anxiety is starting to creep up and you are feeling more anxious than a typical response would warrant, then stop and reward yourself for having recognized this. You are using your new skill of identifying when your anxiety is starting to become unmanageable and this skill is allowing you to continue to tackle and overcome your anxiety.

You can now take practical steps to prevent a relapse, as outlined below.

Be kind to yourself: everybody gets anxious

If you are feeling anxious again, what do you do? First of all, be kind to yourself. We all experience anxiety from time to time and so you are *allowed* to feel anxious. The important thing is that you have recognized your anxiety, which means you are now in a strong position to do something about it. Therefore, rather than tell yourself off for being anxious, acknowledge your anxiety and value your efforts to take the first steps to overcome it.

WHAT HAS LED TO MY ANXIETY?

Remember, you are not 'going back to square one'. Your new skills and experience will protect you from relapse. First, you need to identify what has happened recently that has led to your anxiety. Use the table and example below to help you.

What am I feeling anxious about?	What has happened recently to make me feel this way?	What impact is this having on me?	What would I like to be able to do in this situation instead of feeling anxious?
A presentation at work to a new client	A colleague told me that this new client is very difficult and demanding.	I keep thinking about the presentation and imagining it going wrong. Every time I sit down to prepare I think it will be no good and I feel sick. I am unable to prepare.	I'd like to be able to prepare and feel good about the presentation.

Listen to what anxiety is telling you to do, then do the opposite!
Continue to challenge the anxious thoughts. If anxiety tells you not
to walk into a room, then charge into that room without a backward
glance – yes, you can!

 *Exercise 58*

YOUR RELAPSE PREVENTION WORKSHEET

Use the relapse prevention worksheet below as a guide to remind
you how to deal with anxiety. Keep it somewhere safe so that you
can refer to it whenever you feel anxious.

Include here how you felt when you were facing your anxiety.

→ Before I started this process I felt…

_____

_____

_____

_____

_____

_____

_____

_____

_____

_____

_____

_____

Make a note here of how you feel given the changes you have made and the strategies you have put in to place.

→ Coming towards the end of this book, I feel...

_____

_____

_____

_____

_____

_____

_____

_____

_____

_____

_____

_____

_____

_____

_____

_____

_____

_____

Write here what you wish to continue to aim for in the future. Note situations or circumstances in which you would like to be different, and note any particular goals or forthcoming events that you can work towards.

→ I want to continue working towards·

_____

_____

_____

_____

_____

_____

_____

_____

_____

_____

_____

_____

_____

_____

_____

_____

_____

Note down the potential situations or circumstances that may trigger anxiety in the future.

→ I know that potential triggers for me feeling anxious are…

_____

_____

_____

_____

_____

_____

_____

Write down here all the strategies you have learned. This should act as a summary list of the strategies and how you can use them to tackle the triggers.

→ The strategies I have learned for dealing with these triggers are…

_____

_____

_____

_____

_____

_____

_____

_____

When we feel strong emotions, it can be difficult to think logically and rationally. If you have a pre-written plan, you can simply refer to that rather than have to try to remember everything when feeling anxious.

Use the space below to write out a clear plan of what you will do the next time you feel this way. For example, your plan might be to:

1 step back and consider this from multiple viewpoints

2 look for the evidence of these thoughts

3 set a SMART goal to help you deal with this situation

4 reward yourself and prioritize pleasurable activity.

→ Whenever I feel anxious, I will do the following…

_____

_____

_____

_____

_____

_____

_____

_____

_____

_____

_____

_____

_____

Think about your end goal(s) and what you want to achieve.

→ My motivation for continuing to work on this is…

_____

_____

_____

_____

_____

_____

_____

Write down here key lessons that you have learned. These are not so much specific strategies as more general issues that are important, i.e. 'Take time out for myself', 'Ask for help', 'Remember to reward myself for achievements'.

→ I know it is important that I…

_____

_____

_____

_____

_____

_____

_____

_____

Imagine yourself a year from now, free from anxiety. The aim of this is to give you a longer-term focus and help you picture the future and what you are aiming for.

→ In a year I want to be…

_____

_____

_____

_____

_____

_____

_____

_____

_____

_____

_____

_____

_____

_____

_____

_____

_____

_____

Now imagine yourself five years from now and think about what you would like to be doing in five years' time.

→ In five years I want to be...

_____

_____

_____

_____

_____

_____

_____

_____

_____

'Let us be of good cheer, remembering that the misfortunes hardest to bear are those which will never happen.'

James Russell Lowell

Summary

1 It is normal to experience some anxiety or worry in response to life events but this does not mean that you are 'back to square one'.

2 Remember, you are now more skilled in challenging and overcoming your anxiety than you have been previously.

3 Keep your relapse prevention worksheet somewhere handy so that you can turn to it when you feel anxious.

4 You can overcome this: it is only your anxiety that tells you that you can't. You are stronger than your anxiety.

5 The hard work is done!

What I have learned

→ What are my thoughts, feelings and insights on what I have read so far?

_____

_____

_____

Use the space below to summarize any actions you identify as a result of reading this chapter.

_____

_____

_____

_____

Where to next?

 You have now completed this workbook and your journey out of anxiety. You will have a better understanding of what makes you anxious, what maintains your anxiety and what you can do to help yourself face and overcome your anxiety. Now is the moment to enjoy some time for you. Reward yourself for completing the workbook, wave goodbye to your anxiety and go and relish your life on your own terms – leaving anxiety behind.

Appendices

→ **Appendix 1**

 GOAL-SETTING WORKSHEETS FOR CHAPTER 3

Goal	Specific?	Measurable?	Attainable?	Realistic?	Time-limited?	SMART?

Initial goal:	Specific?	Measurable?	Attainable?	Realistic?	Time-limited?	SMART?

→ Appendix 2

DRAWING YOUR ANXIETY PICTURE FOR CHAPTER 4

Situation that makes me feel anxious:_____

_____

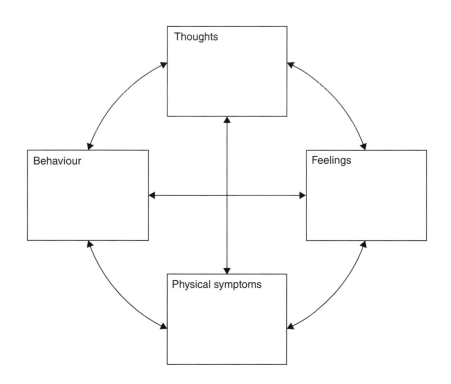

Situation that makes me feel anxious:_____

_____

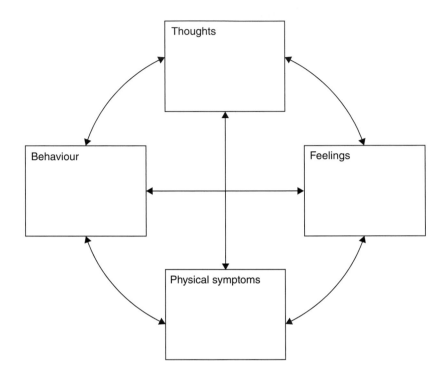

→ Appendix 3

 THOUGHT RECORD SHEETS FOR CHAPTERS 5 AND 9

Situation	Thought	Feelings	Physical symptoms	Behaviour

Situation	Thought	Feelings	Behaviour	Result

→ Appendix 4

BEHAVIOURAL EXPERIMENT WORKSHEETS FOR CHAPTER 6

Behavioural experiment worksheet	
Date and situation	Write down in detail here when and where you were, who you were with, etc.
Key thought being tested: What do you think will happen?	Write down your key thought/belief that is going to be tested here. Rate how strongly you believe this thought/ belief at the time (%).
Experiment: What did you do?	Write down here what you did to test out the thought/ belief.
What did happen?	Write down here what happened during the experiment.
How do you feel now?	Write here how you feel now and anything that you weren't expecting or that surprised you.
Rerated key thought	Re-evaluate that initial key thought/belief and rerate how strongly you believe that thought/belief now (%).

Behavioural experiment worksheet	
Date and situation	Write down in detail here when and where you were, who you were with, etc.
Key thought being tested: What do you think will happen?	Write down your key thought/belief that is going to be tested here. Rate how strongly you believe this thought/ belief at the time (%).
Experiment: What did you do?	Write down here what you did to test out the thought/ belief.
What did happen?	Write down here what happened during the experiment.
How do you feel now?	Write here how you feel now and anything that you weren't expecting or that surprised you.
Rerated key thought	Re-evaluate that initial key thought/belief and rerate how strongly you believe that thought/belief now (%).

→ Appendix 5

CATASTROPHIC THINKING TEMPLATES FOR CHAPTER 7

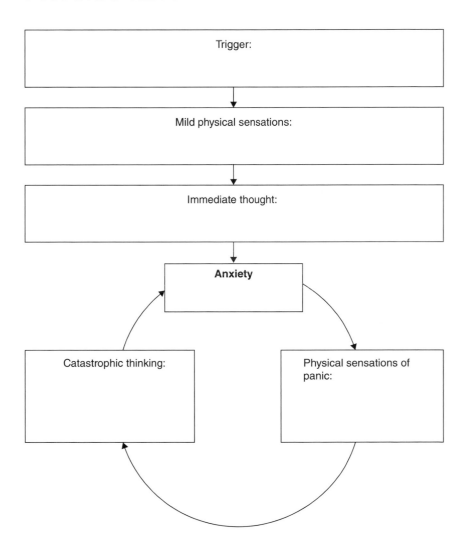

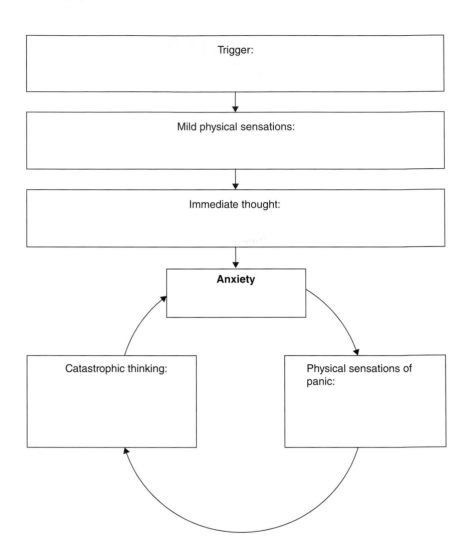

References

Beck, A., *Cognitive Therapy and the Emotional Disorders* (Oxford: International Universities Press, 1976)

Borkovec, T. D., Robinson, E., Puzinsky, T. & DePree, J. A., 'Preliminary exploration of worry: some characteristics and processes', *Behaviour Research and Therapy* (1983), 21, 9–16

Clark, D. M., 'Panic Disorder: from theory to therapy', in *Frontiers of Cognitive Therapy*, P. M. Salkovskis (ed.) (New York: Guildford Press, 1997)

Davis III, T. E., Ollendick, T. H. &. Öst, L-G. (eds.), *Intensive one-session treatment of specific phobias* (New York: Springer, 2012)

Doran, G. T., 'There's a S.M.A.R.T. way to write management's goals and objectives', *Management Review* (1981), 70, 11: 35–6

DSM-IV, American Psychiatric Association, 1994

Foa, E. B., Huppert, J. D., Leiberg, S., Langner, R., Kichic, R., Hajcak, G. & Salkovskis, P. M., 'The Obsessive–Compulsive Inventory: Development and validation of a short version', *Psychological Assessment* (2002), 14(4), 485–96

Freeston, M. & Mears, K., *Overcoming Worry: A self-help guide using Cognitive Behavioural Techniques* (London: Robinson, 2008)

Öst, L-G., 'One-session treatment for specific phobias', *Behaviour Research and Therapy* (1989), 27, 1–7

Öst, L-G., 'Rapid treatment of specific phobias' in Davey, G. (ed.) *Phobias: A handbook of description, treatment and theory* (London: Wiley, 1997), 229–46

Padesky, C. A. & Mooney, K. A., 'Clinical Tip; Presenting the Cognitive Model to clients', *International Cognitive Therapy Newsletter* (1990), 6, 13–14

Purdon, C. & Clarke, D. A., *Overcoming Obsessive Thoughts* (Oakland, CA: New Harbinger Publications, 2005)

Rachman, S., *The Treatment of Obsessions* (Oxford: Oxford University Press, 2003)

Rachman, S. & de Silva, P., *Obsessive–Compulsive Disorder: The Facts* (Oxford: Oxford University Press, 2009)

Salkovskis, P. M., (ed.) *Frontiers of Cognitive Therapy* (New York: Guildford Press, 1997)

Wells, A., 'Meta-cognition and Worry: A Cognitive Model of Generalized Anxiety Disorder', *Behavioural and Cognitive Psychotherapy* (1995), 23, 301–20

Williams, C., 'Use of written cognitive behavioural therapy self-help materials to treat depression', *Advances in Psychiatric Treatment* (2001), 7, 233–40

Wolpe, J., *Psychotherapy by Reciprocal Inhibition* (Stanford, CA: Stanford University Press, 1958)

Useful contacts

Anxiety UK
www.anxietyuk.org.uk/
Anxiety UK
Zion Community Resource Centre
339 Stretford Road
Hulme
Manchester M15 4ZY
Helpline: 08444 775 774 (open Monday to Friday 9.30–5.30)
Admin/office line: 0161 226 7727

OCD-UK
www.ocduk.org
PO Box 8955
Nottingham NG10 9AU
Email: support@ocduk.org
Tel: 0845 120 3778

No Panic
www.nopanic.org.uk
Jubilee House
74 High Street
Telford
Shropshire TF7 5AH
Email: ceo@nopanic.org.uk
Tel: 01952 680460

Mind
www.mind.org.uk
15–19 Broadway
Stratford
London E15 4BQ
Email: contact@mind.org.uk
Tel: 020 8519 2122

The Anxiety and Depression Association of America
http://www.adaa.org/

The International OCD Foundation
http://www.ocfoundation.org/

National Alliance on Mental Illness
http://www.nami.org/

Index